BIRTH INJURY
LAWSUITS
A PARENT'S GUIDE

*A CONSUMER EDUCATION GUIDE BY
THE BIRTH INJURY LAWYERS ALLIANCE*

WORD ASSOCIATION PUBLISHERS
www.wordassociation.com
1.800.827.7903

Printed in the United States of America.

ISBN: 978-1-63385-193-1

Designed and published by

Word Association Publishers
205 Fifth Avenue
Tarentum, Pennsylvania 15084

www.wordassociation.com

1.800.827.7903

TABLE OF CONTENTS

INTRODUCTION & OVERVIEW OF THE MEDICAL MALPRACTICE PROCESS

BIRTH INJURIES: TYPES AND CAUSES

THE MEDICAL MALPRACTICE PROCESS FOR BIRTH INJURIES

AFTER THE TRIAL: NEXT STEPS

FINAL NOTE

RESOURCES

INTRODUCTION & OVERVIEW OF THE MEDICAL MALPRACTICE PROCESS

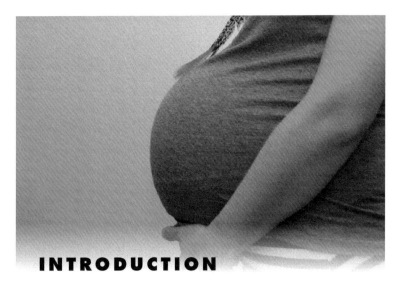

INTRODUCTION

WHAT IS THE BIRTH INJURY LAWYERS ALLIANCE?

by Richard Halpern

You and your partner are starting a family and eagerly anticipate your new arrival. It is a time filled with anticipation, excitement, and some anxiety—but you are ready for it. You seek out skilled and experienced health-care providers to make sure that everything goes according to plan. You read up on what to expect, and you listen to your health-care professional's advice.

The exciting day arrives, and all seems to be going well, but then something terrible happens. Things aren't quite right with your baby. There is pandemonium; you can't get answers to your questions. You're confused. Crushed. Frustrated. Possibly even angry. This is not the happiest time of your life.

You just want to know what happened to your baby and why. The Birth Injury Lawyers Alliance helps to answer these questions and more.

If your child has been injured during the course of labour and delivery and you have concerns with the medical treatment that was provided, it is important that you contact a BILA lawyer as soon as possible. The lawyer will be able to provide you with some preliminary information as to the process of investigating any potential claim and will advise you on the applicable limitation period. There is legislation in each province that limits the amount of time you have within which to issue a claim against the medical practitioners involved.

The Birth Injury Lawyers Alliance (BILA) was formed in 2016 by a group of lawyers from across Canada with considerable experience in birth injury cases to promote the effective representation of children and families affected by avoidable injuries occurring at or around the time of birth. The founding members of BILA practice law in every province and territory in Canada, with the exception of Quebec.

The Birth Injury Lawyers Alliance is a not-for-profit corporation. Its goals are to educate and collaborate to ensure that children suffering from birth trauma get capable and informed lawyers. BILA seeks to facilitate access to justice for these children.

BILA lawyers have largely dedicated their professional lives to representing children and families just like yours who suffer avoidable birth injuries. We recognize that these are complex, heart-wrenching, and challenging cases. When your child has suffered an injury from birth trauma, you and your family will feel vulnerable and emotional.

This book is written by BILA lawyers to help you understand your rights and your child's rights when injury is caused by medical negligence. In it, we'll walk you through the process from retaining a BILA lawyer right up until post-trial (should your case go to trial), outlining what to expect, so you remain informed and aware.

> **Note:** *If your child has just experienced a birth injury, and you don't know where to turn, we are here for you. Everyone deals with stress differently: Some will want to read every bit of information they can find, while others may not be able to process a lot. This guide can be helpful, but we realize it might be too overwhelming for you right now to read an entire book, which is why you'll find a condensed step-by-step action guide at the end of this book (right before the Resource section). This checklist will tell you what you need to know now, and you can return to the guide at a later time for additional information when you feel ready.*

In this book, we will cover the essential things you need to know and consider if you think your child may have been injured by poor medical care at and around birth.

To help you find the information you need when you need it, this book is divided into three main sections.

- Part One gives an overview of what a medical malpractice claim is, the types of injuries that can lead to a claim, and more information on BILA.

- Part Two guides you through the malpractice litigation process, from filing the initial claim to the trial process.

- Part Three discusses what happens after the trial is over and alternative means of action you can pursue. We have also provided a useful Resource section at the end of this book, where you can find information on coping with loss and dealing with a child's disability, as well as a list of BILA lawyers across Canada.

BILA lawyers share access to legal and medical resources to ensure that you and your family receive the highest quality representation and the most current information needed to effectively prosecute your case. Regular communication and contact between the members of BILA is intended to maintain competency in acting for you. No matter who your particular BILA lawyer is, you can benefit from the collective knowledge and experience of all the members of BILA. There is a considerable benefit to having access to this impressive depth and breadth of experience. We'll elaborate further on the many benefits that a BILA lawyer can offer you throughout the book, but here are a few:

- From time to time, BILA holds educational meetings or seminars for lawyers, health professionals, and families affected by birth trauma.

- BILA lawyers make themselves available to present at educational meetings organized by other legal groups, health-care providers, and organizations involved in promoting the interests of affected children.

- BILA members also write regularly on topics of interest to families affected by birth injuries, lawyers, and health-care professionals. Helpful information on a variety of topics is regularly posted to the BILA website (bila.ca).

- We are easily accessible by phone or email to discuss enquiries from families and lawyers about the potential merit of any claim.

On a logistical note, BILA lawyers maintain our separate and distinct legal practices in the provinces in which we reside and practice. We are not partners and are not associated in any other way than that described above. When you are represented by a BILA lawyer, your solicitor–client relationship is with that BILA lawyer and the law firm in which he or she practices. You will not be represented by any other BILA lawyer. When you retain a BILA lawyer, any fee arrangement is with that particular lawyer and his or her law firm. No other BILA lawyer outside that particular firm will participate directly in your case or receive any remuneration.

BILA lawyers understand what parents of injured children go through. We know you worry about your child's future. The costs of looking after a child with disabilities can be substantial. If your child's injuries were caused by a health-care provider's negligence, BILA lawyers believe that the financial burden should be paid by that negligent health-care provider. This guide will help you understand the process of easing that financial burden through a medical malpractice claim.

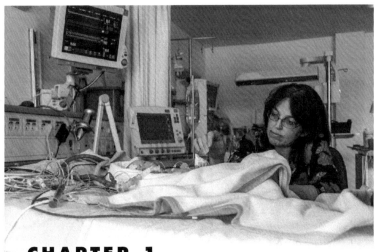

CHAPTER 1

WHAT IS A MEDICAL MALPRACTICE CLAIM?

by Aleks Mladenovic

At the end of a normal pregnancy (at 41 weeks' gestation), Laura's doctor decides to induce labour with Oxytocin. The baby's heart rate is continuously monitored electronically. Progress of labour is slow; at times, the baby's heart rate sounds like it has dropped. Contractions occur frequently. Suddenly, the baby's heart rate lowers and doesn't come back up. The doctors recommend a c-section, and the c-section is completed 45 minutes later. After the baby is born, she needs help breathing. Sometime later, the baby has a seizure. Laura and her husband are told these things happen occasionally and are more often due to things that took place before labour. They are told the baby may have cerebral palsy.

Each year, a small number of babies (but significant in absolute terms) are born in Canada with injuries caused during their birth that should never have happened. If your child is one of these injured babies, you and your child may have a medical malpractice claim.

This book will provide you with some useful information about birth injury claims. In order to better understand birth injury claims, it is important to recognize that a birth injury case is a type of *medical malpractice claim*, albeit a complex one. BILA lawyers have extensive experience with medical malpractice claims in general; they have a *particular* interest in the subset of medical malpractice law that deals with birth injuries.

In general, medical malpractice claims are lawsuits brought by patients and their families against medical professionals (e.g., doctors, nurses, chiropractors, physiotherapists) and medical institutions (e.g., hospitals, private clinics, health-care agencies). These lawsuits are intended to compensate patients and/or the patients' family when substandard medical care results in injury or harm.

In a medical malpractice claim, the burden will be on you to prove that the harm resulted from substandard care. Your BILA lawyer will assemble the proof you need when malpractice occurs.

Medical malpractice claims can arise from virtually any conceivable interaction a patient has with the health-care system. Indeed, preventable injuries from medical care in Canada are more common than most Canadians know. Every year, thousands of Canadians are injured or killed by preventable adverse medical events. Obviously, not all of these adverse events are the result of medical malpractice. Some complications and outcomes are unavoidable. It has been said that medicine is part art and part science. Thus, when it comes to medical care, there is never a guarantee of a perfect outcome, even if the treatment or procedure appears to be routine.

In other words, bad outcomes can occur even with excellent medical care, and not every bad outcome can be blamed on the care providers. However, a significant number of preventable adverse medical events in Canada are caused by the negligence of medical professionals and institutions. These cases are the subject matter of medical malpractice law.

TYPES OF MEDICAL MALPRACTICE CASES

Although every case is unique, there are some general types of malpractice cases that BILA lawyers commonly handle. This list is not meant to be exhaustive, but is intended simply to highlight some common types of medical malpractice claims in Canada:

1. *Birth injury*. These are claims resulting from injuries to mothers and/or babies stemming from events before, during, and after childbirth. These cases are the focus of this book and are discussed in much greater detail in the chapters that follow.

2. *Surgical error*. These are cases arising from injuries caused during or after a surgical procedure. All surgeries carry inherent risks and not all complications are the result of negligence. Some complications are simply unavoidable risks of surgery, and these cases are generally not compensable. However, if the surgical team negligently performs a procedure, resulting in harm to the patient, the patient may have a claim for medical malpractice.

3. *Medication error.* This can involve over-prescription of medication or the prescription or administration of the wrong medication to a patient. The harm caused by this type of error depends on the extent of the reaction to the medication. Some patients suffer relatively mild reactions; for others, the error can be fatal. In the context of birth injury cases, a medication used to increase the intensity and frequency of uterine contractions can be misused.

4. *Diagnostic error.* This involves the failure of a medical professional to correctly and promptly diagnose a patient's condition. If this diagnostic error results in delayed treatment and a worse outcome for the patient, a medical malpractice claim may be justified.

5. *Interpretation error.* These cases involve the negligent interpretation of medical studies or investigations, such as x-rays, CT scans, pathology slides, or blood tests. A radiologist reviews an x-ray and fails to recognize a broken bone or other abnormality, or a pathologist reviews a tissue sample and fails to recognize the presence of malignancy or other disease process. In the birth injury context, this may also involve the negligent interpretation of prenatal ultrasounds.

6. *Referral error.* These cases involve a failure by a medical professional to refer a patient to the appropriate specialist in a timely way. Many times, the first and only doctor a patient sees for a specific medical concern is their family doctor or an emergency room physician. Not all pregnancies are the same; some carry higher risk for both mother and baby and require referral to the appropriately skilled obstetrician. If the patient's condition requires the care of a specialist, a malpractice claim may be justified if the GP or ER doctor

fails to make the referral and the patient's condition is not appropriately managed.

7. *Errors in infection control.* Community acquired infections and the absence of sterile/aseptic protocols can lead to liability of hospitals, doctors, and governmental agencies. In some situations, mothers carry specific bacteria that pose a risk to the baby that requires certain treatment of the mother and monitoring of the newborn.

8. *Informed consent.* Before a patient undergoes treatment, medical or surgical, the medical professional (usually a physician) must provide the patient with meaningful information about the risks and benefits of the proposed treatment. The failure to advise the patient of the material risks of the proposed treatment can form the basis of a malpractice lawsuit. The concept of informed consent is complex, and the law in Canada is evolving. Recent cases have stressed that doctors are obliged to have detailed, meaningful discussions with their patients about treatment options, risks, and benefits. Doctors must not only inform their patients of the material risks of the treatment being proposed, but they must also advise their patients about the risks of *not* having that treatment. In some cases, the failure to properly inform the patient of risk will not give rise to liability where the patient would have agreed to the treatment had they been properly informed. Where a labour is particularly prolonged or complex, there may be an obligation on the part of the obstetrician to offer alternatives to unassisted delivery (e.g., caesarean section).

WHAT ALL MEDICAL MALPRACTICE CASES HAVE IN COMMON

There are two fundamental questions at the heart of every medical malpractice case, regardless of the underlying facts:

1. Did the medical professional(s) meet the *standard of care*? This is another way of asking whether there was negligence in the care provided.

2. If there was negligence, did that negligence cause harm or injury to the patient? This is known as the question of *causation*.

In order to succeed in a medical malpractice lawsuit, you, through your BILA lawyer, must prove both propositions, namely: that there was (1) a *breach of the standard of care*; and (2) that the breach of the standard of care *caused harm or injury*. It is important to understand what these concepts mean and how they play out in the course of your medical malpractice case.

THE STANDARD OF CARE

In a medical malpractice lawsuit, it is not sufficient to show that a decision by a medical professional caused a bad outcome. Mere errors in judgment do not establish liability against doctors, nurses, and medical institutions, even if it results in severe consequences for the patient. You must prove that the actions of the practitioner were below the acceptable standard of care.

The test of whether a doctor or other medical professional breached the standard of care is an objective one. In order to find a breach of the standard of care, a judge or jury deciding a medical malpractice case must conclude that the medical error was one that *no similarly qualified medical professional would reasonably have made in the circumstances.* Essentially, the standard of care is defined by what a reasonable and prudent health-care professional with similar qualifications would have done in the same circumstances.

The standard of care is not fixed or static. It will vary from case to case depending on a number of factors, including:

1. *The qualifications of the medical professional being sued.* Because doctors and other health-care professionals have different areas of practice, different levels of specialty training, and different levels of experience, not all medical professionals will possess the same level of skill, knowledge, or experience. For example, a family doctor does not have the same expertise in treating tropical diseases as would an infectious disease specialist. The family doctor would, therefore, not be held to the same standard as the infectious disease doctor in that regard. Similarly, the standard of care expected of an obstetrician delivering a baby would not apply to a midwife or even an obstetrical nurse. In other words, when it comes to the standard of care, the test is what a similarly situated and trained medical professional would reasonably be expected to know and do in the circumstances. Despite these principles, where a health-care provider assumes responsibility for a patient's care that she or he should know is beyond their skill set, the courts may hold them to a higher standard.

2. *The clinical scenario.* The standard of care may change depending on the acuity, severity, or risk of the clinical situation. In cases where there is a greater risk of harm to the patient, greater vigilance and, therefore, a higher standard of care may be required.

3. *Where the care is being rendered.* The standard of care may also depend on where the treatment is being given. Thus, the standard of care at a small rural hospital may be different than what is expected at a large urban centre, equipped with the latest modern technology and facilities.

CAUSATION

Even where you can prove a breach of the standard of care, you must also establish that this breach actually caused harm or injury. This is known as the issue of *causation*, and in medical malpractice cases, causation can be complex and difficult to prove. Many medical malpractice cases have been lost on grounds of causation even though the plaintiff has proven that the care was below standard. Causation is a particularly challenging issue in birth injury cases, where the medical issues are complex, and there are often competing theories about the mechanism and timing of the baby's injuries.

In order to prove causation, you must demonstrate that your child would not have sustained the injury or harm *but for* the substandard care. The burden of proof is on you to establish causation on a *balance of probabilities*—it must be more likely than not that with appropriate care, the injury would have been avoided or mitigated. Scientific certainty is not required to prove causation, but there must be more than just the loss of a chance or opportunity for a better outcome.

While it may initially seem obvious that the injury was caused by the substandard care at issue, defence lawyers and their experts routinely argue that other causes were at play. For example, in a birth injury case where a baby sustains neurologic injuries that become evident after birth, the defence may argue that the injuries were caused by factors that preceded labour and delivery.

This may include genetic conditions or metabolic abnormalities. Alternatively, the defence may argue that the injuries occurred so late in the labour and delivery that nothing could have been done to avoid injury to the baby.

This issue of the timing of injury is an important theme in medical causation. The debate involves the timeliness of care and whether earlier diagnosis and/or intervention would have made a difference to the outcome. We see this theme not only in birth injury cases, but also in most cases involving delayed diagnosis, where there is a window of opportunity to optimize the patient's well-being or prognosis. You must establish that on a balance of probabilities (greater than 50% probability), earlier diagnosis and treatment would have resulted in a better outcome—either less injury or avoidance of injury altogether.

As already mentioned, timing of injury is a crucial question in most birth injury cases. This is true particularly when the allegation is that the obstetrical team failed to expedite the baby's delivery despite evidence of fetal distress. You must prove that your baby's injuries occurred at a time *after* the delivery should have been effected. This can be difficult to prove in many cases. Fortunately, BILA lawyers have done a great deal of research into causation issues in birth injury cases.

Some members of the obstetrical community in Canada and the United States have written protocols and guidelines that have made it even more challenging for you to prove causation in birth injury cases. These guidelines have been successfully used in court to shield doctors, nurses, and hospitals from liability in birth injury cases, even when the care itself is found to be below the accepted standard. Again, BILA lawyers have made considerable inroads into exposing the flaws in the medical literature that might be used inappropriately to deny some children the compensation they deserve.

THE ROLE OF EXPERTS

Ultimately, it is up to a judge or jury to decide whether there were breaches of the standard of care that caused your baby harm or injury. However, in making these findings, courts rely on the evidence of expert witnesses who testify at trial on behalf of plaintiffs and defendants. Only expert medical witnesses can provide opinion evidence regarding the issues of standard of care and causation at trial, and only after they have demonstrated that they have the proper qualifications to do so.

Given the importance of expert evidence, choosing which expert to retain is one of the most important decisions your medical malpractice lawyer will make. A number of factors are considered when selecting an expert for a medical malpractice lawsuit:

1. *Qualifications.* The expert must have the background, experience, and training to opine on the issues in the case. In a birth injury case, your BILA lawyer will likely consult with obstetricians and nurses who will provide their opinions on the care that was provided. A variety of experts may be consulted in regard to causation, including neonatologists, paediatric neuroradiologists, neurologists, geneticists, and placental pathologists.

2. *Objectivity of the expert.* A good expert will be unbiased and free of conflicts of interest. Even the most qualified expert will not be of much value if a court perceives that he or she is not objective, honest, or fair. The expert should not have preconceived notions about the care that was provided; he

or she must not be seen to favour one side or the other. Unfortunately, some experts have gained reputations for siding with either plaintiffs or defendants in medical malpractice cases. Relying on such experts may make it more difficult to settle the case or succeed at trial because of the expert's perceived bias or lack of credibility.

3. *Ability to testify in court.* Some experts simply make a better impression than others when it comes to writing a report or testifying at trial. An expert may be well-credentialed and unbiased, but the impact of his or her evidence will usually be blunted if he or she is incapable of distilling his or her opinion convincingly in a report or in the witness box. It is, therefore, crucial to retain an expert who is not only qualified, but who can also be trusted to deliver his or her opinion in a way that is understandable and persuasive to a judge or jury. These intangible qualities in an expert witness can make the difference between winning or losing a medical malpractice lawsuit, where the judge or jury is routinely presented with "duelling experts" and must decide which expert to believe.

DAMAGES

If you can establish liability against a medical professional for malpractice, then you and your family may be entitled to financial compensation for the injury or harm they sustained. This compensation is known as *damages* and represents the "value" of your case. Any award of damages is intended to restore the victim of malpractice to the same position (financially speaking) that he or she would have been in but for the negligent care, insofar as money can do. Thus, damages are generally viewed as a form of *restitution* for the plaintiff, not punishment for the defendant. In very rare cases, the conduct of a medical professional may result in an award of *punitive, exemplary or aggravated damages*, but this is only where the conduct is extreme (i.e., reckless or intentional). Damages are discussed in more detail in Chapter 8.

The value of the damages in a particular case may be a factor when you are considering a medical malpractice claim. These cases are vigorously defended. Significant resources are available to physicians and hospitals to defend these claims in court. Moreover, the lawyers who represent hospitals and physicians in malpractice matters are highly trained and experienced in this area of the law. This means that you need to have experienced malpractice lawyers on your side. It also means that your malpractice lawyers must invest significant resources and time to successfully advance your interests. As a result, commencing a lawsuit when the injuries (and therefore the damages) are modest may not always be in your financial interest. BILA lawyers understand these complex issues and will provide you with guidance and advice regarding the costs and benefits of proceeding with a medical malpractice claim. Often damages in birth injury cases are quite substantial, highlighting the importance of pursuing these cases.

Medical malpractice is a complex and challenging area of law. In pursuing a case for medical malpractice, it is important to keep in mind that the issues of standard of care and causation are highly technical from both a medical and legal perspective. The value of the underlying case itself may determine whether a particular malpractice claim is viable. The success of any malpractice action will depend on the underlying merits of the case, as well as the skill and experience of the birth trauma malpractice lawyer and the experts that he or she retains.

Birth injury litigation is a particularly complex subset of medical malpractice law. Indeed, birth injury lawsuits may be the most complex and challenging of all the types of medical malpractice claims. Consequently, having the appropriately skilled lawyer to represent you is an important factor that will improve your chances of success.

BIRTH INJURIES: TYPES & CAUSES

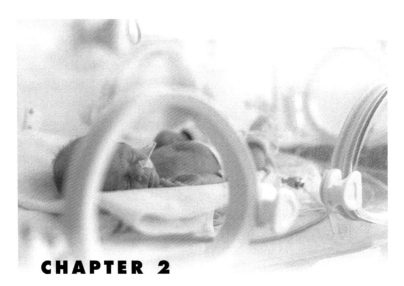

CHAPTER 2
WHAT KIND OF INJURIES CAN LEAD TO A CLAIM?

by Joe Miller

Immediately after delivery, Mary's baby looks pale and does not cry. Mary is not allowed to hold her newborn right away and watches as they put a tube down the baby's throat before whisking him away. Some hours later, while Mary is trying to breastfeed her baby, he turns pale again and tenses up. The doctors tell her the baby had a seizure. Later, Mary is told that the seizure could have been caused by poor oxygenation of the baby's brain some time before birth that might have caused permanent injury to brain tissue.

In the majority of cases that lead to a medical malpractice claim, the baby suffers a brain injury. The brain injury can result from a disruption of blood flow to the baby's brain, a stroke, or a hemorrhage (bleeding), and it can occur before labour, during labour and delivery, or in the period following birth (neonatal period).

This chapter will review these types of brain injury claims, as well as other types of obstetrical/neonatal claims, including injuries to spinal column nerves arising from shoulder dystocia and injuries arising from treatable genetic conditions.

BRAIN INJURIES

Oxygen deprivation during labour and delivery

Hypoxic ischemic encephalopathy (HIE) simply means brain sickness from inadequate oxygenation to the brain. The fetus receives his or her necessary oxygen and nutrients from the mother through the umbilical cord. If this delivery mechanism is compromised, the baby may suffer an irreversible neurological injury.

Contractions during labour may result in a reduction of blood flow through the umbilical cord, causing a reduction in the delivery of oxygen and nutrients to the fetus. When a contraction ends, the blood supply through the umbilical cord usually returns to normal. In the vast majority of situations, the fetus can tolerate the momentary reduction in blood supply and recovers during the resting phase in between contractions. In some cases, however, the repeated reduction in the supply of oxygen and nutrients during contractions will exceed the reserves of the fetus and, if this pattern continues, can result in neurological injury. Babies that are growth restricted, or are preterm, have lower reserves and are less able to tolerate the reduction in blood supply. If labour is induced or augmented with Oxytocin, this can cause longer, more frequent contractions, reducing the time between contractions and limiting the baby's ability to recover.

In the case of twins, a transfer of blood between twins (referred to as twin-to-twin transfusion) can occur, which reduces the ability of one or both twins to tolerate the stress of labour.

One of the responses of the fetus to the decrease of blood flow is a change in the fetal heart rate and its pattern. Electronic fetal monitoring (discussed more in Chapter 3) is used to detect any changes in the fetal heart rate or pattern that suggests that the fetus is not tolerating labour and to allow for intervention prior to neurological injury occurring. It is the responsibility of both nurses and doctors to respond to any evidence of impaired fetal oxygenation suggested on the fetal heart tracing. By doing so, injury to the baby can, in some circumstances, be avoided or mitigated.

Some situations cause the fetal blood supply to decrease suddenly and significantly: uterine rupture during an attempt at a vaginal birth after cesarean, cord prolapse, placental abruption, and shoulder dystocia. This profound decrease in the blood flow will result in a significant decrease in the fetal heart rate—a sign that the baby needs to be delivered immediately.

Periventricular Leukomalacia

This brain injury occurs in some premature babies. The more premature the baby, the higher the risk of this injury occurring. In medical terms, this is an injury to the white matter of the brain around the ventricles. The premature baby does not have a fully developed system for the supply of blood to all parts of the brain. In addition, the premature baby has not fully developed its autoregulation system, which is the body's mechanism to regulate blood pressure throughout one's body to maintain adequate blood flow and, therefore, oxygenation, to the brain. This makes a premature baby vulnerable to changes in blood pressure, which compromises the blood flow to parts of the brain and can result in irreversible neurological injury.

Intraventricular Hemorrhage

Similar to periventricular leukomalacia, this condition can also affect premature babies. The immature blood vessels and the lack of a developed autoregulation system puts a premature brain at risk of hemorrhage with any significant changes in blood pressure or neonatal infections.

In Utero Stroke

Strokes can result from a blockage of blood flow or a bleed in the brain. Strokes commonly affect one side of the baby's brain, whereas a brain injury due to oxygen deprivation usually affects both sides. The critical issue when stroke causes a brain injury is to determine the cause of the stroke, which, in some cases, can be linked to episodes of lack of oxygen during labour.

Trauma due to vacuum or forceps

While the risk is small, injuries such as retinal hemorrhage and hematomas can result from the use of vacuums and forceps. As a general rule, it is not recommended to use both forceps and vacuum to deliver a baby, and the obstetrician must be prepared to proceed to cesarean section if the baby cannot be delivered using either forceps or vacuum.

Hypoglycemia

Brain cells require both oxygen and nutrients, including glucose, to live. Some babies are born at risk of having a glucose imbalance. A small baby, sometimes referred to as being intrauterine growth restricted (IUGR), and large fetuses, sometimes referred to as macrosomic or large for gestational age (LGA), are at significant risk of having a glucose imbalance. Further risks include maternal diabetes and gestational diabetes. In utero, the fetus receives its glucose from his or her mother. The concern with neonatal hypoglycemia arises after birth when the newborn baby is required to regulate his or her own blood sugars. If this ability is compromised, the failure of the newborn to effectively be able to provide the necessary glucose may result in death of brain cells, resulting in an irreversible neurological injury.

Kernicterus

Kernicterus is a type of brain injury that can result when a newborn has severe jaundice. Left untreated, a substance in the blood called *bilirubin* accumulates and spreads into the brain tissue resulting in permanent brain damage. There are risk factors associated with the development of kernicterus, including premature birth, problems with breastfeeding, and the development of jaundice in the first 24 hours after birth. Once diagnosed, most jaundice is easily treated with regular feeding and light therapy.

Infection

A newborn baby, particularly a small or preterm baby, is at risk of suffering a neurological injury if he or she catches certain infections. The mother may be carrying Group B Strep bacteria, which can be passed on to the baby as the baby is delivered. As well, infection can occur during labour, affecting the placenta (*chorioamnionitis*) or the umbilical cord (*vasculitis* or *funisitis*). These conditions may have an impact on the health of the newborn.

Phenylketonuria (P.K.U.)

In Canada, babies are tested for a number of genetic conditions. Many of these conditions, including phenylketonuria (P.K.U.), are easily treatable. But if left untreated (perhaps due to mislaid test results), irreversible brain damage can occur.

NON-BRAIN INJURIES

By John McKiggan

Brachial Plexus Injury and Erb's Palsy

A brachial plexus injury is an injury to the nerves in the neck of the baby caused by attending to shoulder dystocia, an obstetrical emergency. When a baby is at a position where his or her umbilical cord is pinched closed, due to where the baby is in the birth canal, the obstetrician must deliver the baby within minutes of the shoulder dystocia occurring or else risk the possibility of neurological injury due to the interruption of the blood flow through the umbilical cord to the baby.

A brachial plexus injury can occur when the obstetrician applies downward traction on the fetal head in an attempt to dislodge the shoulder. This downward traction can stretch the nerves in the baby's neck and, in extreme examples, can result in avulsion of the nerve, meaning that the nerves are pulled away from the cervical spine. Brachial plexus injuries are often temporary but, in some unfortunate situations, they can be permanent. This injury to the brachial plexus nerves will have a direct effect on the functioning of the arm on the side where the nerve injury occurred.

There are three different types of brachial plexus injuries that are dependent on the amount of force applied to your baby's shoulder:

- **Neuropraxia:** This type is injury is caused when scar tissue builds up around a nerve after it has been pulled, stretched, or torn. The scar tissue interferes with the ability of the nerve to transmit nerve signals. Surgery can remove the scar tissue and restore nerve function.

- **Rupture:** This happens when the brachial plexus nerve is torn. In order to correct a ruptured nerve, a surgeon will have to do a nerve graft, which links the gap created by the torn nerve.

- **Avulsion:** This is the most serious form of brachial plexus injury and is known as *Erb's Palsy.* An avulsion injury happens when the root of the nerve is completely torn away from the spinal cord. This type of injury typically requires a complete nerve graft in order to create a new nerve path.

Some Erb's Palsy injuries may heal on their own some may require surgery to repair. Some children can be left with significant life-long disabilities. Erb's palsycan cause weakness and disability in the shoulder, arm, and hand. Many Erb's palsy injuries can cause permanent paralysis of the arm and shoulder.

Some of the risk factors that can lead to shoulder dystocia and Erb's palsy:

- A prior delivery where the baby had shoulder dystocia
- Use of drugs like Pitocin or Syntocin to speed up labour
- Moms who have diabetes

- Larger babies (greater than 8.4 lbs.)

- Moms who have a small pelvic opening (*cephalopelvic disproportion*)

- Long labour

- Breech (feet first) position

- Baby's head turned the wrong way during delivery

If patients present with these risk factors, doctors may deliver a baby early and/or perform a scheduled c-section. Should no risk factors present and should dystocia occur, there are a number of techniques or maneuvers a doctor can use to safely deliver the baby. But, as described above, there is also the possibility of an injury occurring during the process.

Other conditions

In some rare situations, a fetus can be subjected to medications taken by his/her mother at a critical time in fetal development, which can result in birth defects. The treatment of newborn complications, if not done properly, can lead to a claim.

During labour and delivery, health-care practitioners rely on their expertise and certain medical tools to alert them of a problem. The next chapter gives more information on an important monitoring tool: the Electronic Fetal Monitor (EFM).

CHAPTER 3

ELECTRONIC FETAL MONITORING: WHY IS IT IMPORTANT TO THE SAFETY OF YOUR BABY?

by John McKiggan

Near the end of Joan's labour, her contractions come fast and furious. She hears the constant beep of the baby's heartbeat on the monitor. Early in the labour, the beeping of the baby's heart rate seemed consistent and regular, but now, each time Joan experiences a painful contraction, she hears the baby's heartbeat slow and then speed up after her contraction is over. The nurses seem to be paying extra attention to this and even call for the doctor, but no one tells Joan or her partner why they are suddenly more attentive. Just before delivery, the baby's heartbeat slows but doesn't speed up again. When the baby is born, she isn't breathing.

As noted earlier in this book, hypoxic-ischemic encephalopathy (HIE) is a condition of newborn brain sickness that can be caused by impaired oxygenation of a baby during labour and delivery. Unfortunately, this can lead to brain injury and profound physical and cognitive disabilities, including cerebral palsy (which involves motor dysfunction and cognitive challenges) and neuro-developmental problems (that might cause learning disabilities and behavioural issues).

HIE is caused by an impairment of oxygenation to the brain related to issues with the placenta and/or issues with the umbilical cord. The fetus is supplied with oxygenated blood through the uterus to the placenta and through the umbilical cord; the umbilical cord is attached to the placenta. Any condition that impairs the flow of blood to the placenta (for example, uterine contractions) or to the umbilical cord (like compression of the cord) has the potential to impair oxygenation to the fetus.

A healthy and well-grown fetus has considerable capacity to tolerate intermittent interruptions in oxygenation, particularly if any episodes of impaired oxygenation are separated by adequate rest and recovery. This capacity to tolerate the normal stresses of labour is often referred to as *fetal reserve*. Fetal reserve is not, however, unlimited. If episodes of impaired oxygenation are allowed to go on too long, or are too severe, fetal reserve can be depleted and, eventually, exhausted. Some babies may come into labour with less fetal reserve, particularly babies who might have been growth restricted (small babies) during pregnancy.

During labour and delivery, a baby's well-being is assessed by nurses and doctors by monitoring its heart rate. There are features of the fetal heart rate, when interpreted properly, that can suggest a possible problem with fetal oxygenation. The most important tool that doctors and nurses use to measure a baby's oxygenation during labour and delivery is the Electronic Fetal Heart Monitor (EFM).

WHAT DOES THE EFM DO?

The Electronic Fetal Monitor provides a continuous tracing of both the fetal heart rate (FHR) and uterine contractions. The nurses and obstetricians use this tracing to see if the pattern reflects a fetus that is well-oxygenated or a fetus that may be under a degree of stress due to impaired oxygenation.

In the case of any atypical patterns, a change to the approach to managing the labour may be required in order to protect the health of the baby. The FHR patterns must be interpreted in the context of the uterine activity, as well as the stage and progress of labour.

The data on the EFM is a crucial factor in determining whether the injury occurred during labour and delivery and whether the standard of care required some other approach. BILA lawyers have spent a considerable amount of time studying the issues concerned with FHR patterns and the impact the EFM data has on proving liability.

HOW DOES THE EFM WORK?

The EFM monitor has two devices that detect pressure called *transducers*. The transducers are placed on the mother's abdomen and held in place with straps. From time to time, it may be necessary for the nurses to adjust the transducers in order to achieve an adequate signal to produce a clear and continuous heart rate tracing on the recording strip.

The EFM has a screen or monitor that shows the fetal heart rate. The EFM also produces a printed strip of paper that is covered in grids showing time segments and heart rate. Data from the EFM monitor is plotted on the strips and looks like two wavy or spiky lines. A properly trained professional can tell a great deal about the well-being of a fetus during labour by looking at these lines. The top line represents the fetal heart rate. The line spikes up or dips down to reflect changes in the fetus' heart rate. The bottom line shows the mother's uterine contractions. The line peaks when she is having a contraction.

EFM monitors also produce sounds that are related to the fetal heart rate. An alarm sounds when the fetal heart rate is too fast or too slow.

UNDERSTANDING EFM DATA

It is important that the nurses and physicians caring for the mother and fetus are properly trained in the use and interpretation of EFM data. There are a number of different factors that the EFM monitor will record that are critical to evaluating the baby's health and well-being.

Contractions

One of the transducers measures the pressure produced during a contraction. The EFM will detect the duration of the contraction (how long it lasts) and the frequency of the contractions. A normal pattern for contractions is every 2 to 3 minutes and not more often. The nurses or doctors monitoring the labour will assess the intensity of the contractions by feeling the mother's belly. They are also required to ensure that the uterus relaxes between contractions.

When contractions come more frequently than every 2 minutes, it is called *tachysystole*. The risk of tachysystole increases when physicians use certain drugs (e.g., Oxytocin) to try to induce or augment labour. Contractions that last for a duration longer than 90 seconds are called *hypertonic* or *tetanic* contractions.

The problem with contractions that occur too frequently or that last too long is that they can contribute to impaired oxygenation of the baby. These uterine contraction patterns extend the time of stress on the fetus, increasing the risk of diminishing fetal reserve. Concerning fetal responses to these kinds of uterine contractions may be seen as changes in the pattern of the fetal heart rate.

Fetal Heart Rate (FHR) patterns

The Society of Obstetricians and Gynecologists of Canada has established guidelines defining the important data collected by the EFM. Unfortunately, some of these guidelines fail to provide adequate guidance on how to respond to some fetal heart rate (FHR) patterns in the context of all the clinical circumstances. BILA lawyers are familiar with the current guidelines and have an understanding of the shortcomings.

Baseline: The baseline is the average of how fast the fetus' heart beats over a period of 10 minutes (beats/minute). The normal baseline for a healthy fetus is between 110 and 160 beats per minute.

- If the heart rate goes above 160 beats per minute for extended periods of time (more than 10 minutes), this is a condition known as *tachycardia*. Tachycardia may be a sign of fetal distress.

- When the heart rate drops below 110 beats per minute, this is called *bradycardia*. Bradycardia is a sign of fetal distress, and it usually means the fetus is not getting enough oxygen.

Variability: Variability refers to the oscillation of the FHR above the baseline and dips below the baseline. A healthy fetus' heart rate usually fluctuates over time, so it is normal and reassuring to see variation in the heart rate.

- If the oscillation in the heart rate is greater than 25 beats per minute, the variability is classified as *marked*.

- Variability that ranges between 6 and 25 beats per minute is classified as *moderate*.

- Variation of less than 5 beats per minute is classified as *minimal*.

- When the heart rate is traced essentially as a flat line, the variability is classified as absent.

A healthy fetus will normally produce a heart rate with moderate variability. If FHR variability is minimal, it can be due to a number of factors. Sometimes medication administered to the mother can reduce variability. Fetal sleep can be a cause as well. Finally, minimal variability can be caused by impaired fetal oxygenation and, therefore, is cause for concern. Absent variability and marked variability are both non-reassuring.

The obstetrical care providers need to consider all the clinical circumstances and medical evidence to determine whether reduced variability is something that is normal and not of any concern or whether the reduced variability is a non-reassuring sign of potential fetal distress.

Accelerations: Sometimes the EFM monitor will show abrupt spikes in the heart rate. An abrupt increase in the heart rate of more than 15 beats per minute is referred to as an acceleration. Accelerations are often normal and a reassuring sign that the baby is doing well. Having said that, accelerations occurring in the context of other atypical or abnormal FHR patterns cannot be considered reassuring.

Decelerations: A dip in the heart rate below the baseline is referred to as a deceleration. There are different kinds of decelerations, each with slightly different significance for assessing fetal well-being. In addition to the various patterns and timing of decelerations, the depth and duration of a deceleration is clinically significant. Decelerations of longer duration and deeper depth are more concerning.

- **Early decelerations** are a gradual decrease in the fetal heart rate that typically mirrors the mother's contractions. This type of decrease in FHR is thought to be caused by head compression from a contraction. While many obstetrical texts and journal articles consider early decelerations to be normal and benign, there is more recent literature suggesting that no deceleration is entirely benign. As well, there is reason to believe that head compression has the potential to be harmful to the fetus when excessive or prolonged.

- **Variable decelerations** are an abrupt drop in the fetal heart rate of more than 15 beats per minute lasting anywhere from 15 seconds to 2 minutes. Variable decelerations are commonly seen during labour and are thought to be caused by umbilical cord compression. Variable decelerations are categorized as either uncomplicated or complicated.

- *Uncomplicated variable decelerations* show an initial spike (acceleration) then a dip (deceleration), followed by another spike (acceleration) before the heart rate returns to the normal baseline. Uncomplicated variable decelerations that occur repetitively may be a sign of fetal intolerance to labour and intermittent decreased fetal oxygenation. The frequency, depth, and duration of these decelerations are important for determining the degree of distress being experienced by the fetus.

- *Complicated variable decelerations* may have loss of variability in the deceleration, may be a deceleration in two phases, or may be a deceleration that takes a long time to return to the baseline. Complicated variable decelerations are concerning and can be a sign of fetal distress.

- **Late decelerations** is when the bottom of the deceleration occurs after the peak (or tip) of the contraction tracing. Late decelerations are generally accepted by medical professionals to reflect some degree of *hypoxia* (oxygen deprivation) in the fetus.

- **Prolonged decelerations** are decelerations that last for more than 2 minutes. These decelerations are concerning and require immediate clinical action from the obstetrical team.

EFM classification

When a nurse or doctor looks at the EFM strip, they have to consider all of the circumstances and all of the data on the monitor in order to classify the tracing.

It used to be that EFM strips were categorized as either *reassuring* (the information on the monitor showed that the baby was doing well) or *non-reassuring* (the information on the monitor suggests the baby may not be doing well). Unfortunately, this easy-to-understand classification system has been abandoned by the medical profession. In recent years, the Society of Obstetricians and Gynecologists of Canada created new guidelines to categorize EFM strips as *normal, atypical,* or *abnormal.*

- **Normal** EFM strips are considered to represent a well-oxygenated fetus and are generally what was once referred to as a reassuring tracing. In other words, the baby is likely to be happy and healthy.

- **Abnormal** tracings contain data that strongly suggest that there are problems with fetal oxygenation and that the baby may be at risk of injury. Abnormal tracings usually require immediate action either to try to address the cause of the abnormal tracing or to expedite delivery of the baby by c-section or operative vaginal delivery (e.g., forceps, vacuum).

- **Atypical:** Unfortunately, most EFM tracings fall into the atypical category. This category of tracing is poorly defined and consists of a FHR pattern that is neither normal nor abnormal. These types of tracings suggest that there may or may not be a problem with fetal well-being and expedited delivery may or may not be required. The appropriate response to an atypical tracing depends on a consideration of the entire clinical context in which it occurs and is usually the subject of much debate in birth injury malpractice claims.

EXPERT EVIDENCE

One of the first things that your birth injury malpractice lawyer will do is hire an obstetrical expert to assess the fetal heart monitor tracings. That expert will be asked to determine whether there was any evidence of fetal distress and whether the obstetrical team responded appropriately to the available data.

Experienced birth injury malpractice lawyers have some degree of skill in understanding and interpreting EFM tracings to determine whether there are potential grounds for concern and whether it is appropriate for further investigation by hiring a medical expert.

THE MEDICAL MALPRACTICE
PROCESS FOR BIRTH INJURIES

CHAPTER 4
WHY HIRE A BILA LAWYER?

by Paul McGivern and Susanne Raab

Pauline Smith, age 30, enjoyed a healthy pregnancy before going into spontaneous labour at full term (40 weeks). Everything seems normal at first, but then the labour drags on for many painful hours. Towards the end of the labour, there seems to be some concern for the fetal heart rate, but no one discusses that with Pauline or her husband, Todd. Immediately after the birth, the baby isn't breathing and is whisked away. Pauline and Todd are told that their daughter may later have cerebral palsy and this sometimes happens for unknown reasons. They want to investigate the reason for their baby's injury, so they hire a BILA lawyer.

There's no shortage of lawyers to be found, so you might wonder why you should hire a BILA lawyer. The answer is simple: to level the playing field.

In the field of birth injury, the playing field is far from level. Physicians in Canada are represented by an organization called the Canadian Medical Protective Association (CMPA), a highly sophisticated and well-funded organization. Its mission statement (found on their website: CMPA-camp.ca) includes "protecting the professional integrity of physicians," and they defend these physicians vigorously.

A quick glance at the CMPA's most recent annual report[1] reveals some frightening statistics. In 2014, of all of the medical malpractice cases that were heard in court, the plaintiff (injured person) lost and received no compensation in 72% of the cases. Of the cases that resolved out of court, 60% resulted in dismissals, again with no compensation to the plaintiff. It is worth pointing out that previous years have seen even more dismal outcomes for injured plaintiffs.

BILA lawyers will handle your case in a way that improves the odds of success. Importantly, these statistics *do not* reflect the experience of BILA lawyers. BILA lawyers have a track record of success in representing victims of medical malpractice, particularly children with birth injuries.

There can be no doubt that the CMPA is a formidable foe, with many advantages in its favour. BILA lawyers, however, are committed to creating a level playing field. We do so through our experience, hard work, and collaboration. We share knowledge, resources, and information. We develop strategies and work together to advance the law in the areas where we

---

1). CMPA-camp.ca

perceive unfairness to children living with cerebral palsy and other birth trauma injuries. We have dedicated our professional careers to learning the highly specialized law and medicine involved in birth injury cases and building a network of medical experts prepared to give the type of objective, unbiased opinions necessary to succeed with these cases.

While BILA lawyers have a lot of experience in handling birth trauma cases like yours, the collaboration between BILA lawyers across Canada provides access to the depth of experience that may not be available elsewhere.

When you are looking for the most capable and experienced lawyer to handle your child's case, there are some important questions you should ask.

- How many birth trauma cases have you handled? (BILA lawyers, collectively, have handled hundreds of these cases.)

- What do you do to keep up with the latest developments in obstetrics, neuroradiology, and neonatology? (BILA lawyers attend and speak at conferences on these issues regularly. BILA lawyers also maintain an extensive library on these subjects.)

- Have you taken a birth trauma case to trial? (BILA lawyers have taken many of these cases to trial.)

- How are you going to access the experienced medical experts needed to prove my case? (BILA lawyers regularly deal with outstanding experts in all the important medical fields.)

- Can you read and interpret what is in the hospital records and the fetal heart rate tracing? (BILA lawyers have spent thousands of hours learning to read and interpret medical records and fetal heart tracings.)

Your case is important. Don't be afraid to ask any questions you wish and expect direct answers.

While BILA lawyers represent a wide range of medical malpractice victims, they have a *particular* interest in birth injury claims. All BILA lawyers have extensive, hands-on experience with birth injury litigation.

CHAPTER 5

WHAT CASES WILL BILA LAWYERS ACCEPT?

by Aleks Mladenovic

Risa and Jack are shocked to learn that their daughter may have cerebral palsy. Risa's pregnancy had been normal, and she had taken good care of herself. But she was not happy with the care she received during her labour. Risa and Jack speak to a friend about investigating whether something went wrong during her labour but are told that suing doctors in Canada is too difficult and expensive, and the patient is rarely successful. Doctors have considerable resources to fight lawsuits, and Risa and Jack are facing huge expenses to look after their daughter. They are at a loss as to what to do.

Every birth injury case is unique. Each has its own particular set of facts and challenges that sets it apart from others. It would, therefore, be impossible to describe every single scenario that might give rise to a birth injury claim. However, it may be useful to discuss, in general, the types of birth injury claims BILA lawyers will accept.

Many of the medical issues described below were highlighted in Chapter 2; however, this chapter will dig a little deeper into explaining how these situations factor in when a BILA lawyer accepts your case.

CEREBRAL PALSY AND OTHER NEUROLOGIC INJURY CAUSED BY DELAYED DELIVERY

Sadly, a common type of birth injury claim is one involving neurologic (brain) injury to a newborn caused by the failure of the obstetrical team (doctors, nurses, midwives) to intervene or expedite delivery in the face of fetal distress. If the baby is incapable of tolerating the intrauterine environment for whatever reason, an urgent delivery by caesarian section or other means may be necessary. The failure to deliver the baby promptly in these circumstances can lead to oxygen deprivation, a condition known as *hypoxia*.

Severe or prolonged hypoxia can lead to decreased blood supply to the baby's organs, called *ischemia* and can result in permanent injury to the baby's brain and other vital organs. As discussed previously, *hypoxic-ischemic encephalopathy* (HIE) is a condition involving injuries to a baby's brain caused by lack of oxygen (*encephalopathy* simply means brain sickness). Babies with these types of injuries may later develop permanent neurologic conditions such as *cerebral palsy* (CP) or other cognitive and developmental problems. Although CP has a variety of other causes, a significant number of CP cases can be attributed to impaired oxygenation during labour and delivery.

A number of factors can lead to this type of injury. These include, but are not limited to:

1. Umbilical cord compression
2. Abnormal uterine contractions, particularly those occurring too frequently or lasting too long
3. Shoulder dystocia
4. Low blood pressure in the mother (maternal hypotension)
5. Rupture of the uterus
6. Placental abruption
7. Excessive pressure on the baby's head during uterine contractions

The obstetrical team is charged with monitoring fetal and maternal well-being during labour and delivery. They can monitor the fetus' well-being using a variety of surveillance techniques, including electronic fetal heart monitoring (EFM). As explained in Chapter 3, EFM provides clues about how the fetus is tolerating the contractions and the stresses of labour. If a fetus is deprived of oxygen, this will cause changes in the heartbeat; these changes will be evident on the EFM tracing.

Warning signs on EFM tracings must be heeded by the obstetrical team. The failure to intervene in the face of worrisome changes on the EFM tracing can result in serious injury to the baby, including HIE. Such medical errors can form the basis of a successful birth injury claim.

BILA lawyers will often accept cases in which the obstetrical team failed to expedite the delivery, despite what should have been apparent concerns from the EFM tracing and other clinical information. In other words, the failure to perform an urgent or emergency c-section or to deliver the baby by other operative means may give rise to a birth injury claim.

FAILURE TO PROGRESS DURING LABOUR AND DELIVERY

A birth injury claim may be warranted where the obstetrical team failed to perform or arrange a timely c-section or other operative delivery despite an excessively lengthy labour. During childbirth, the obstetrical team should monitor the rate of dilatation of the mother's cervix as well as the position of the baby and its rate of descent down the birth canal. In some cases, the labour may be excessively slow to progress; in other cases, there may be no progress at all.

There are a variety of reasons to explain the failure of labour to progress: there may be mechanical issues related to the baby's position or presentation, the baby's head may be too large for the mother's pelvis, or the uterine contractions may not be effective in pushing the baby out through the birth canal. Regardless of the reason for the lack of progress, the obstetrical team must be vigilant in assessing progress and deciding when to intervene. In some circumstances, steps will need to be taken to either increase the contraction with drugs or else deliver the baby operatively on an urgent or emergent basis. Sometimes a natural vaginal delivery may not be possible or safe. In those circumstances, it is necessary for the obstetrician to consider either an operative vaginal delivery (i.e., the use of forceps or vacuum) or a c-section.

Allowing the labour to continue for a long time without progress may give rise to a birth injury claim. This is particularly the case if the second stage of labour (after full cervical dilatation) is prolonged. In a prolonged second stage of labour, the waves of contractions, together with the mechanical forces of the mother's pelvis on the baby's head may lead to neurologic injury or death.

Labours that last too long can injure the mother's uterus as well. Some women experience post-partum haemorrhage following an unduly prolonged labour. If severe enough, this can lead to the need to surgically remove the uterus (hysterectomy) and even death. In addition to preventing further pregnancies by hysterectomy, this operation also brings on premature menopause.

OXYTOCIN USE

BILA lawyers frequently handle cases involving the imprudent use of Oxytocin. Oxytocin, also known as Pitocin or Syntocin, is a medication commonly used to initiate or augment labour and expedite delivery. Oxytocin accomplishes this by stimulating the uterus. In so doing, Oxytocin causes the uterus to contract more frequently and with greater intensity, hopefully causing more rapid cervical dilatation and descent of the baby in the birth canal. When properly administered, Oxytocin is a valuable and important tool for the obstetrical team. Problems arise when too much Oxytocin is used or when the obstetrical team fails to recognize that the Oxytocin negatively affects the health of the baby or mother.

As previously mentioned, a normal, healthy baby is usually able to tolerate the stresses of labour, including the stress of uterine contractions. Problems may arise if contractions become too frequent, a condition known as *tachysystole* or *uterine hyperstimulation*. Oxytocin is a medication that is known to cause hyperstimulation of the uterus when used in excess. Too much Oxytocin can result in waves of contractions that effectively reduces the baby's oxygen supply. Without enough time to recover between contractions, the baby begins to deplete its reserves. If this continues, the baby's reserves become dangerously low and the baby will decompensate, eventually resulting in hypoxic-ischemic injury.

Given the potential for Oxytocin to hyperstimulate the uterus, it is imperative that the obstetrical team carefully administer it, monitoring the dosage and the mother's and baby's response. If there is evidence of uterine hyperstimulation or worrisome changes on the EFM tracing, Oxytocin should be tapered or discontinued to prevent injury to the baby and the mother.

In addition to the indirect impact of Oxytocin on the baby's oxygen supply, Oxytocin may also indirectly result in rupture of the uterus, a condition that poses a grave risk to mother and baby.

In short, the imprudent use of Oxytocin may form the basis of a birth injury claim, and BILA lawyers are frequently consulted on such cases.

SHOULDER DYSTOCIA

In a normal vaginal delivery, the baby's head emerges first, followed shortly thereafter by the shoulders. In rare cases, one or more of the baby's shoulders may be trapped behind the mother's pelvic bone, preventing delivery. This is known as *shoulder dystocia*. Without an effective and rapid response by the obstetrical team, shoulder dystocia can lead to serious injury to the baby's arm and shoulder. In some cases, it can also lead to brain injury and death.

Trapped behind the mother's pelvic bones, the baby's shoulder is vulnerable to tugging forces. Pulling on the baby's head or neck in an effort to free the shoulder may cause damage to a delicate cluster of nerves in the baby's arm, known as the *brachial plexus*. Brachial plexus injuries can result in *Erb's Palsy,* a permanent neurologic condition. Children with Erb's Palsy may have lifelong disabilities, including paralysis in the affected arm.

In extreme cases, the failure to deliver the baby because of shoulder dystocia can lead to oxygen deprivation and asphyxia.

Given the potential complications from shoulder dystocia, the obstetrical team must respond quickly and skillfully. There are a number of maneuvers the obstetrical team should perform in the presence of shoulder dystocia. Each of these maneuvers is intended to free the shoulder from the mother's pelvic bone, including the McRoberts maneuver, whereby the mother's legs are flexed and her thighs are brought towards her abdomen. The obstetrician can also reach inside the vagina in an effort to manually rotate the baby's arm free, a technique known as the Wood's Corkscrew maneuver. The obstetrical team can also press down on the mother's lower abdomen in an effort to push the baby's shoulder clear of the pelvic bone.

If the obstetrical team fails to carry out one or more of these maneuvers in a timely and skillful way and the baby suffers harm, this may form the basis of a birth injury claim.

In some cases, the obstetrical team should be prepared for the possibility of shoulder dystocia or other mechanical problems. This is particularly true when the baby is large or there are other physical reasons to expect a difficult delivery. Risk factors include:

1. Baby is past the expected date of delivery

2. Lengthy labour with slow descent or slow dilatation of the cervix

3. The baby is large for gestational age

4. Gestational diabetes

5. Small or petite mother

6. A mother with a narrow pelvis

In some cases, the failure of the obstetrical team to anticipate a difficult vaginal delivery and recommend alternatives may form the basis of a birth injury claim.

NEGLIGENCE IN ANTENATAL CARE

Obstetrical malpractice is not limited to medical errors made during labour and delivery. There is a duty of care throughout the course of the pregnancy.

It goes without saying that negligent antenatal (prenatal) care can result in injury to the mother or baby. In some cases, where there is inadequate screening or counselling for genetic abnormalities such as Down Syndrome (Trisomy 21), parents may be deprived of their right to decide if they want to proceed with the pregnancy at all. In other cases, the failure to properly manage maternal problems such as high blood pressure or diabetes can lead to serious complications that put the life of the mother and baby at risk.

Good antenatal care requires the use of various modalities and screening tests to assess the health of the mother and baby. This means regular fetal surveillance and assessment by way of blood tests, ultrasonography, EFM, and, in certain circumstances, amniocentesis and genetic testing. If a baby is born with genetic abnormalities or conditions that were not adequately screened for during the pregnancy, the parents may have a claim for the extraordinary costs of caring for and raising that child.

It is likewise essential that the health of the mother be regularly monitored during pregnancy. Maternal blood pressure, in particular, must be carefully monitored and controlled. Failure to do so may lead to *preeclampsia*, a condition characterized by high blood pressure and damage to the mother's kidneys. Preeclampsia is a serious condition that may be a threat to the life of the mother and baby.

Maternal glucose levels should be routinely monitored throughout the pregnancy. Up to 10% of all pregnant mothers will develop some degree of *gestational diabetes*, a condition characterized by diminished insulin response resulting in increased blood sugar levels. Without appropriate screening, diet, and medical management, gestational diabetes can result in complications for the mother and her baby. For example, gestational diabetes may result in a baby who is too large for a safe vaginal delivery. Untreated, gestational diabetes may also increase the risk of preeclampsia, seizures, and stillbirth.

NEGLIGENCE IN NEONATAL CARE

BILA lawyers also accept cases involving substandard neonatal care, which involves the care a baby receives after delivery. Depending on the baby's condition at birth, a wide range of care requirements may come into play. If the delivery was difficult or complicated, a neonatal team may be required to resuscitate and treat the baby immediately at birth. The failure to have that team present at the time of delivery may raise questions about the quality of care.

A baby who is born after a difficult delivery may require ongoing care in a critical care setting, such as a neonatal intensive care unit (NICU). The baby may require ultrasound, CT, or MRI brain imaging. The baby may require transfer to a paediatric hospital. If the baby has suffered a hypoxic-ischemic brain injury, treatment with hypothermia (cooling) and other forms of management may be necessary to minimize the harm. Should the baby develop seizures, these will need to be quickly treated to avoid further neurologic injury. All of these complex issues may be the subject of a birth injury claim.

NEGLIGENCE IN C-SECTION OR OPERATIVE DELIVERY

A variety of problems can occur during a c-section or operative vaginal delivery (i.e., forceps, vacuum). In some cases, the outcome from the operative delivery may raise questions that warrant investigation by a BILA lawyer.

A negligently performed c-section may result in injuries to the mother, including injuries to her bladder, uterus, blood vessels, and other vital organs. Lacerations and injuries to the baby are also possible.

Delivery by forceps likewise carries risks to both mother and baby. Negligent use of forceps may result in injuries to the mother's bladder, urethra, and perineum. Risks to the baby include cranial fracture, facial fracture, and lacerations or injuries to the facial nerves. In rare cases, the baby may suffer brain injury or death.

DEATH OF MOTHER OR BABY

In some cases, the process of labour and delivery, or complications during pregnancy, may result in the death of the mother or baby. These heart-wrenching cases usually involve the same issues seen in cases of maternal or fetal injury. The issues of standard of care and causation must be investigated in order to determine if a valid malpractice claim exists.

As this chapter demonstrates, virtually anything that goes wrong during pregnancy or labour and delivery can raise questions about the quality of medical care. The only way to know if a malpractice claim exists is to properly investigate the facts and medical-legal issues involved. If you or your family have questions or concerns about the medical care you received during pregnancy or the birth of your child, a BILA lawyer will be able to advise you of your legal rights and whether a claim should be advanced.

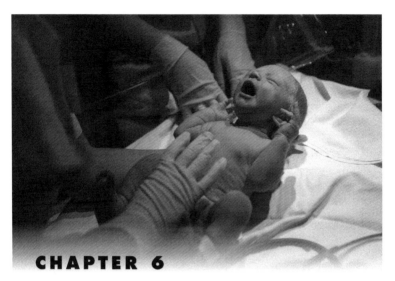

CHAPTER 6

HOW DO I FIND OUT WHAT HAPPENED TO MY BABY?

by Joe Miller

The doctor who delivers Jennifer's baby at the community hospital was one Jennifer had never met before. After delivery, the baby has difficulty breathing and is whisked off to a larger hospital with a neonatal intensive care unit. Jennifer never receives an explanation from the doctor who delivered her baby about why her baby was born in such a depressed condition. She doesn't even remember her name.

You may not know exactly what caused your baby's injuries. You may suspect that something went wrong, but no one has explained what happened. Or you may only know that your child has disabilities with no explanation of a cause. Even where there has been some disclosure by the doctors about what happened to your baby, many parents still have many unanswered questions. They often face a stone wall when asking for answers from health-care providers, either because they do not know the answer or they are afraid of the consequences of providing the answer.

Your BILA lawyer can help get these questions answered. Sometimes, parents will not know the precise questions to ask; fortunately, BILA lawyers know which questions to ask and who to ask.

The first step to finding out what happened to your baby is to obtain the medical records. Health-care professionals have a duty to record what happens during the care of a patient. You have a right to obtain your medical records and those of your child. If you have hired a lawyer to investigate a potential case, that lawyer can do that for you. All you will need to do is sign authorization forms allowing them to do so on your behalf.

There are many different kinds of medical records that provide valuable information about what happened to you and/or your baby. The clinical notes and records from your prenatal doctor show the health of you and your baby before labour and delivery. The mother's chart from the hospital gives information about how well the baby tolerated labour while in the womb and whether there were any complications during the labour and delivery process. The baby's chart from the hospital shows any complications the baby had after he or she was born. Importantly, experienced birth injury lawyers always obtain copies of the actual imaging (MRIs, CAT scans, and ultrasounds) taken during pregnancy and the newborn period, including images of the newborn's brain after birth. These are crucial test results that need to be reviewed to assess your case.

Once your lawyer receives your medical records, he or she will review them, a task that can be difficult unless you have experience with these type of records. It is easy to miss something important if you are not used to working with medical records—abbreviations and acronyms are commonly used in medical records, so most people do not understand what is written. The heart rate of your baby in utero is often tracked electronically, and these records are vitally important to determine what happened but are meaningless to someone who has never looked at electronic heart rate tracings before. A BILA lawyer knows what to look for in the records, is familiar with fetal heart tracings, and is particularly knowledgeable about the significance of certain entries in those records.

To determine what happened to your baby, birth injury lawyers aim to answer two main questions:

1. Was somebody negligent?

2. Did that negligence cause an injury to the baby?

Your BILA lawyer will carefully review all the relevant medical records to identify the issues of importance and the questions to be asked of the medical experts. Answering these questions will involve feedback from experts (e.g., obstetricians, neurologists, neuroradiologists). Those experts look at the antenatal records, labour and delivery records, and imaging to form an opinion on what happened. The opinions of these experts must be coordinated and agree in order to make the necessary connection between the substandard care and the harm.

Understandably, the main issue of concern for most parents is to get a clear explanation for what happened to their baby. Once that issue is resolved can you decide whether you can, and wish to, hold a health-care professional accountable.

CHAPTER 7

IS MY CLAIM WORTH PURSUING?

It is clear that three-year-old Billy is not reaching expected milestones. He was slow to walk, and he knows only a few words. The paediatrician has not explained exactly why this is happening. Genetic testing is normal. Billy's delivery was stressful, and his parents are looking for answers. They are wondering if they need legal representation.

If your child has been injured during the course of labour and delivery and you have concerns with the medical treatment that was provided, it is important that you contact a BILA lawyer as soon as possible. The lawyer will be able to provide you with some preliminary information as to the process of investigating any potential claim and will advise you on the applicable limitation period. There is legislation in each province that limits the amount of time you have to file a claim against the medical practitioners involved.

While each lawyer's procedure may vary somewhat in terms of the investigation of a potential claim, there are a number of steps that you can expect. These include the following:

1. Initial interview
2. Obtain medical records and other information (discussed in Chapter 6)
3. Careful review of the records to identify the medical-legal issues
4. Retain medical experts
5. Potential consultation with other BILA lawyers
6. Preliminary assessment of damages
7. Meet to discuss claim assessment and if litigation is warranted

INITIAL INTERVIEW

Your BILA lawyer will want to meet with you in person to conduct an initial interview about the events leading to your child's injury. However, if you do not live in or near the same city as a BILA lawyer, this interview can take place over the telephone. Your lawyer will ask you questions about your medical history, your obstetrical history, and particulars of the pregnancy and delivery in question. He or she will want details of your prenatal care, together with the names of physicians involved. The lawyer will then ask you detailed questions with respect to the progress of your labour and delivery. It is important to provide as much detail as possible with respect to all individuals involved and any discussions that you had with health-care professionals during labour. In advance of this meeting, if you are able, it is helpful for you to write out a detailed chronology of the events as you remember them. This will help your BILA lawyer prepare for the first meeting, understand your case, and serve as a way to refresh your memory of events later on in your case.

Your lawyer will be interested in the condition of your baby at delivery and what medical procedures and assessments have been performed since the birth. The lawyer will also want to know the names of the physicians and other health-care professionals who provided care to your child.

During this initial interview, your lawyer will advise you on the process involved in pursuing a medical malpractice claim, as well as the process involved in investigating to see whether a claim is warranted.

In some instances, your lawyer may provide a retainer agreement in relation to the initial investigation, so that you are able to consider whether you wish to retain him or her to proceed with the investigation.

OBTAIN MEDICAL RECORDS AND OTHER INFORMATION

Once you and your lawyer have agreed to proceed with an investigation into the potential claim, your lawyer will need to have access to all of the relevant medical records. In some situations, you may be able to obtain these directly from the health-care professionals and hospitals involved. In other cases, your lawyer will have you sign authorization forms permitting his or her office to request the relevant medical records on behalf of you and your child. At a minimum, it is usually necessary to obtain the records of:

• the prenatal care

- any attendance at hospital for non-stress tests during the course of the pregnancy

- all of the records for labour and delivery

- all newborn records and brain imaging relating to the baby

If your first consultation with your BILA lawyer is some time after your baby was born, it will be necessary to obtain records relating to all the medical care and diagnostic evaluations since initial discharge from hospital.

In some situations, your lawyer may want to obtain written accounts of the memories of other people who were present during the labour and delivery, such as family members. This will depend on the nature of the events and whether independent recollections as to events and discussions will be critical to an assessment of the claim.

RETAIN MEDICAL EXPERTS

In order to succeed with a medical malpractice claim, it is essential to prove four elements:

1. That the medical professional owed you and your child a duty of care

2. That the medical professional breached the applicable standard of care

3. That your child and family suffered injury and damages

4. That the breach of the standard of care is the legal cause of the injury and damages.

In order to properly investigate a birth injury claim, it is always necessary to obtain independent medical opinions with respect to the standard of care and causation issues.

Standard of care experts

In order to obtain an opinion on the standard of care, your lawyer will first locate an appropriately qualified physician (or other health-care practitioner) who is willing to perform the independent review. Typically, the standard of care expert is an obstetrician. BILA lawyers have considerable access to these experts as a result of their work in other cases like yours. Your lawyer will provide the relevant medical records to the expert for his or her review, along with a letter summarizing the facts and issues in the case.

BILA lawyers, through their experience in birth injury cases, have the ability to identify and analyze the medical-legal issues in your case. This is crucially important in their interactions with the expert consultants in order ensure that the right questions are asked and properly addressed by the expert. In this way, your BILA lawyer can properly test and scrutinize the opinions of the expert consultants to ensure that your case has been thoroughly and fairly evaluated on the merits.

Once the expert has reviewed the records, he or she will meet with your lawyer to discuss his or her opinion on the appropriate standard of care and whether the medical practitioners met the required standard of care during the course of the labour and delivery. In some cases, a written report may immediately follow, but this will depend on the situation and the individual practice of your lawyer.

Depending on the nature of the events, assessing the standard of care issue may require retaining a nursing expert together with either a family physician or obstetrician (depending on the qualifications of the physician responsible for the delivery). In general, it is important to obtain a supportive opinion from an independent expert who has the same or similar qualifications to those who were involved in the delivery in question.

For example, if the delivery occurred in a small rural hospital and was overseen by a family physician, your lawyer will generally want to obtain an opinion from a family physician who does obstetrics work, particularly one who has experience working at a smaller hospital. While courts have moved away from the previously accepted idea that there is a different standard of care in rural and urban areas, there is certainly still a difference in the availability of resources between those centres. As such, it is generally important to seek an opinion from a similarly stationed expert.

By way of further example, if you had a high-risk pregnancy and the physicians involved were highly qualified specialists, your lawyer will want to obtain an opinion from similarly qualified physicians in a high risk obstetrics unit. The standard of care applicable to each medical practitioner is the standard of a reasonably competent health-care professional of similar qualifications.

Causation experts

Proving what caused your child's injuries is often a complex issue in birth injury cases. Your lawyer will need to locate experts who are highly qualified and current on the relevant medical literature to provide an opinion as to the nature of the injury sustained by your child, the timing of the injury, and, most importantly, its cause. In medical malpractice cases, plaintiffs do not need to establish the cause of an injury beyond a reasonable doubt. To the contrary, the civil burden of proof is "on a balance of probabilities." This means that you will require an expert who is able to say that it is "more likely than not" (more than 50% likely) that the cause of your child's injury was the care provided by the medical practitioners involved.

The type of experts who may be required to provide causation opinions could include pediatric neuroradiologists, neonatologists, pediatric neurologists, geneticists, or other specialists depending on the circumstances and the nature of the injury.

Obtaining an opinion on the timing of your baby's injury is crucial in many cases and involves some careful analysis by the expert and a considerable body of medical literature. To succeed in these claims, the expert expressing an opinion with regard to timing of injury must be able to say that the injury occurred *after* the breach of the standard of care. Only in this way can we prove that, had the standard of care been met, the injury would have been avoided.

POTENTIAL CONSULTATION WITH OTHER BILA LAWYERS

As stated earlier, one of the benefits of retaining a BILA lawyer to investigate and potentially prosecute your claim arising from a birth injury is that he or she will have the ability to consult with other BILA lawyers in relation to your claim. In some instances, your lawyer may have a strong sense that there should be a viable claim arising from a particular set of circumstances. However, in some of those situations, the initial experts that are retained may not provide supportive opinions.

In those circumstances, a consultation with another of the BILA lawyers may be useful in identifying another possible expert or an alternate theory of causation. This can be invaluable in permitting the case to move forward despite the initial unsupportive opinions.

PRELIMINARY ASSESSMENT OF DAMAGES

As indicated above, another essential element that must be proven is that damages resulted from your child's injury. Birth injury cases typically require expert consultation in order to assess the damages of the infant into the future. However, at the stage of the initial consultation and investigation, it is usual for the lawyer to perform a preliminary assessment of the damages issues. This may involve looking at previously decided cases or gathering further information from you as to your child's prognosis and likely future needs. (It may be too early at this stage; to accurately predict your child's future needs; however, this is something that will be assessed in greater detail as the matter progresses, should it be determined that the case warrants proceeding with a lawsuit.)

MEET TO DISCUSS CLAIM ASSESSMENT AND IF LITIGATION IS WARRANTED

Once your lawyer has completed the above steps, he or she will likely arrange a meeting with you to discuss his or her assessment of the case. While there are never any guarantees of success in medical malpractice cases, including birth injury cases, your lawyer will advise you as to his or her opinion of the merits of your potential claim, based on his or her experience, the medical records, expert opinions, and consultations with other BILA lawyers.

Your lawyer will recommend whether you should proceed with an action. This will involve a detailed discussion as to the legal and medical issues involved in your case, together with the legal process should you proceed with a claim. Your lawyer will also discuss with you the fee arrangements that will be required. There is no fee unless and until your claim is successful. All BILA lawyers offer their clients the option of proceeding on a contingency fee arrangement. This means that you will not pay your lawyer for his or her time as the matter progresses, but rather, your lawyer will receive a percentage of the recovery if the matter is successfully resolved, either through settlement or after trial.

In some instances, your lawyer may recommend that the matter be referred to one of his or her colleagues within BILA. This may depend on the ability of a particular firm to conduct the matter on an appropriate fee arrangement or may be due to the particular skills of one of the other BILA members.

After your BILA lawyer evaluates your case, he or she will then be in a position to make recommendations to you about whether you should proceed with a lawsuit against any health-care professionals who may have provided substandard care that caused your baby's injury.

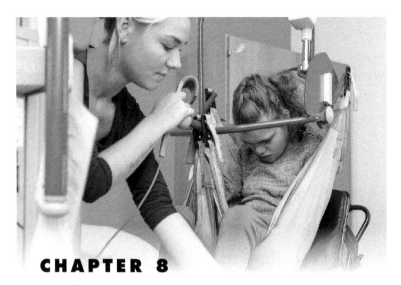

CHAPTER 8

HOW IS MY CHILD'S COMPENSATION CALCULATED?

by Paul McGivern and Susanne Raab

Rachel and Jason filed a medical malpractice claim against their doctor for injuries their daughter sustained when the Oxytocin Rachel was given during labour caused their baby to be deprived of oxygen for too long. Their daughter, now two, has cerebral palsy and requires significant daily medical help. In addition, Rachel and Jason will soon have to renovate their home to make it wheelchair accessible for their daughter.

Rachel and Jason have spent two years caring for the daughter round-the-clock. The financial stress and anxieties they have about their daughter's quality of life have left them physically and mentally exhausted. They long to take a family vacation.

After a three-week trial that relied heavily on expert testimony and reviewing Electronic Fetal Monitoring records, Rachel and Jason are awarded a settlement that will cover the medical care their daughter requires, the necessary home renovations, loss of income for both their daughter and Rachel (who now must stay at home full time to care for her daughter), as well as damages pertaining to the pain and suffering the couple have endured.

Like most parents, you might be motivated to pursue a medical malpractice lawsuit following a birth injury to obtain the financial resources necessary to provide for your child. Children with cerebral palsy, for example, have significant, lifelong needs and the public system is wholly inadequate in providing the level of care and support required. You might be struggling with limited public resources, support, and services, and often, there is no choice in the process. You're exhausted, having to advocate at every turn to obtain the most basic services for your child. You worry about who will provide for your child when you are no longer able.

While financial compensation does not solve all of these challenges, your ability to choose and fund the best support and services available for your child can make all the difference in your child's life. It provides opportunities for growth and development, lightens the load, and reduces the financial, physical, and emotional stress associated with providing for a disabled child. While no amount of money can ever heal your injured child, having the financial resources to pay for the proper care and rehabilitation of your child can help provide you with some peace of mind about your child's future.

The purpose of a lawsuit is to obtain that funding. When the injury has been caused by negligence, financial compensation will often also give you your lives back. Proper funding allows for sufficient outside support so you can go back to work (if you wish to do so), volunteer outside the home, have a social life, and have a life again with your spouse (if applicable).

In this chapter, we will review the main categories of compensation that may be available for a child living with cerebral palsy in a successful medical malpractice matter. Of course, no two cases are alike, nor even are two children with cerebral palsy. The amount of compensation any given child is entitled to receive will depend on that child's unique needs, abilities, and circumstances.

Please be aware that this is not an exhaustive list, rather it is intended to provide a general overview of the most significant areas of compensation. Differences also exist between the various provinces across the country.

COST OF FUTURE CARE

This is the most important category of compensation. It is meant to provide you and your child with the money needed to put your injured child in the position he or she would have been in had he or she not sustained the injury. In other words, it is supposed to provide sufficient funds to pay for the care needs of your child throughout his or her lifetime.

If the injury is severe enough, your child may require ongoing medical care or assistance long after being discharged from hospital and perhaps for a lifetime. Parents of children injured at birth know all too well that these children have extraordinary care needs. The financial, physical, and emotional burdens of caring for children with birth injuries are overwhelming. Caring for these children often requires around the clock vigilance, with no respite for the family. Even with government assistance and services, most families struggle to cope. Parents usually end up providing most of the care themselves, at great personal expense and sacrifice. They worry about what will happen to their children if and when they are no longer able to care for them. Few families can afford to purchase the care and services their injured children need now, let alone over the course of a lifetime, an expense that could easily be in the millions of dollars.

Fortunately, there is no limit to the amount a court can award for the cost of care. The court is entitled to award as much as is necessary to ensure that the injured child receives the care and services they need, for as long as they may need it.

The process of determining what amount of compensation should be provided to your child involves a number of assessments by appropriately qualified experts, such as (in the case of a child living with cerebral palsy) a pediatric physiatrist (physician who specializes in the rehabilitation of children), a pediatric neuropsychologist, an occupational therapist, a physiotherapist, and a speech language therapist. An expert qualified as a life care planner prepares a comprehensive report listing all of the various supports, services, and equipment that will be required to provide for the child for his or her entire lifetime, as well as associated costs.

In practical terms, in the context of a birth injury resulting in cerebral palsy, compensation typically includes the following:

- *Attendant care.* This covers the costs of hiring a support worker during the day and/or night to provide the child with the additional care and support required due to his or her disability, as well as the costs of housekeeping and home maintenance services. For a child with a severe birth injury, this may include home care by nurses or personal support workers. Where family members provide some or all of the extraordinary care, they are entitled to be compensated at a rate that reflects the fair market value of the care they provide.

- *Therapy.* This includes the costs of all therapy the child may require over his or her lifetime (e.g., physiotherapy, occupational therapy, speech language therapy, psychological therapy, aquatic therapy, hippotherapy).

- *Case management.* This includes the costs of a caseworker, often a nurse or occupational therapist, who plans and organizes the various supports and services required for the child.

- *Equipment.* This covers the costs of the wide variety of equipment and technological devices a child living with cerebral palsy may benefit from (e.g., wheelchairs, a wheelchair-accessible van, lift systems, adapted sports equipment, communication devices).

- *Medical supplies and medication.* This covers the costs of items such as feeding equipment, hygiene supplies, and medication.

- *Home modifications/purchases.* This covers the costs of either renovating the child's current home to make it fully accessible for the child or, alternatively, if it is not possible to renovate the current home, it covers the additional costs associated with building or purchasing an accessible home (e.g., lifts, ramps, grab bars, railings).

- *Other.* In addition to the above, compensation may include the costs of any other item or service recommended by an expert.

LOSS OF INCOME/LOSS OF INCOME EARNING CAPACITY

Each child diagnosed with cerebral palsy is affected differently. Some children with cerebral palsy grow up and find gainful competitive employment with earnings similar to what they would have earned without any injury. These people will have a limited (if any) claim for compensation under this category.

For many children, however, the combination of physical challenges, communication barriers, cognitive limitations, fatigue, and/or numerous medical and therapy appointments make finding competitive employment as adults simply unrealistic. Their focus, instead, is typically on finding meaningful and enjoyable ways to contribute to their communities through volunteer opportunities. In these circumstances, their claim for compensation for the loss of their ability to earn income as a result of their disability is significant.

Compensation for loss of income is calculated by comparing the amount of income the person would have earned had they not suffered their injury with the amount of income they will be able to earn with their injury (if any). In the case of a birth injury, it is generally assumed the child would have attained a level of education and earnings similar to what their parents and/or siblings achieved, had he or she not been injured at birth.

NON-PECUNIARY DAMAGES ("PAIN AND SUFFERING")

This category of compensation is meant to compensate an injured person for their physical and emotional pain and suffering. While the previous categories of compensation are meant to reimburse the injured person for the financial costs associated with their injury, this category of damages is meant to provide an additional fund of money to be used to provide solace to the injured person for what they have lost. Damages for pain and suffering are also known as *general damages*.

In Canada, general damages are awarded based on the nature and severity of the underlying injury. Although there are no hard and fast rules about how much to award for any particular injury, Canadian judges and juries rely on *precedent*, meaning they tend to award general damages along a range or spectrum established by previous court decisions involving similar injuries. This means that when a judge or jury decides how much to award for general damages in a particular case, they will likely consider what courts in the past have awarded in cases involving similar injuries. The same considerations apply when the two sides of a malpractice lawsuit are negotiating a settlement out of court. Since no two people are exactly alike and no two cases are identical, it will always be possible to distinguish prior cases from the case at hand. Still, prior case law is an important consideration when assessing general damages for pain and suffering.

In the late 1970s, the Supreme Court of Canada placed an upper limit on the amount of compensation allowable under this category of damages of $100,000 (other monetary claims are not limited). The court's concern at the time was that this was a difficult claim to quantify and did not rely on any objective measure. The court observed that no amount of money could possibly truly compensate a person for the pain and suffering associated with a catastrophic injury, and they feared an escalation of the amount of compensation awarded under this category, as has occurred in the United States of America.

This upper limit of non-pecuniary damages has increased over time to reflect inflation and is, at the time of writing, approximately $365,000. In deciding what amount of compensation an injured person is entitled to receive, the court will consider a variety of factors, including the injured person's age, the nature of the injury, the severity and duration of the pain, the level of disability, and the loss of lifestyle or impairment of life. A child living with cerebral palsy as a result of a birth injury is typically entitled to be compensated at, or close to, the maximum allowable amount of damages.

CLAIMS OF FAMILY MEMBERS

Immediate family members of patients injured by medical malpractice may have claims of their own. Immediate family members are spouses, parents, children, siblings, grandparents, and grandchildren of the injured patient. In many cases, these family members provide care and services to the injured plaintiff, for which they can receive compensation. Family members can also be compensated for money they have spent to purchase care and other services that would not have been required but for the injury to their loved one.

Immediate family members can be compensated for the loss or change of the relationship that results when their loved one is injured or killed as a result of medical malpractice.

OTHER CATEGORIES OF COMPENSATION

In addition to the above, compensation may also be available for:

- the parents' time spent in relation to providing for their child's disability-related needs up to the time of settlement/judgment

- the child's lost opportunity to form an interdependent relationship and benefit from the associated cost sharing of co-habitation

- the professional services of a financial planner and/or corporate trustee to invest and manage the settlement/judgment funds to ensure it is properly invested and lasts for the entirety of the child's life

Damages in birth injury cases are often amongst the highest awards in all personal injury cases. This results from the considerable care needs of children with serious neurologic injury.

When your BILA lawyer is successful in recovering a substantial damages award for your child, great care is taken to ensure that the funds are carefully invested and protected so that your child's future is secure even when you may no longer be able to take care of them. This goes a long way to providing you with peace of mind.

CHAPTER 9

WHEN IS A TRIAL NECESSARY?

by Aleks Mladenovic

Maureen and George know something had gone terribly wrong when their son is born and doesn't cry. They are told that he suffered a lack of oxygen and the pediatrician immediately cooled his whole body using hypothermia. The doctors are very apologetic for the baby's condition, but it appears that he responded well to the cooling. Though their baby is doing well, they wonder about his future.

The vast majority of birth injury claims that BILA lawyers take on will be settled out of court, without the need for a trial. BILA lawyers accomplish this in a number of ways. BILA lawyers carefully investigate all potential cases to ensure that only meritorious claims are advanced. There is no incentive to advance a claim if a breach of the standard of care cannot be proven or if the necessary causation cannot be established through expert witnesses or if the costs of pursuing the claim will be more than the potential recovery.

BILA lawyers will bring all of their skill, resources, and experience to bear in an effort to resolve your birth injury claim as efficiently and effectively as possible.

There are two main reasons that a trial may be necessary: either the defence simply refuses to settle the case or else the parties cannot agree on the settlement amount. These reasons are discussed below.

DEFENDANT REFUSES TO SETTLE

A settlement requires the agreement of both parties. In exceptionally rare cases, the plaintiff will instruct his or her lawyer not to settle the claim. This rarely happens in birth injury cases, since most medical malpractice victims are simply seeking compensation for their child's injuries and are content to resolve the matter out of court.

The same cannot be said of all defendants. In some cases, the defence will take a firm position on a case and will not agree to settle the claim for any amount. When this happens, it is usually because the defence believes they have a strong, defensible case on the merits. This may relate to either the standard of care, causation, or both.

In medical malpractice cases, defendants or their lawyers will often take a so-called *principled approach*, meaning they will only settle those cases where there is a real risk that a court will find in the plaintiff's favour. If the defence is able to deliver strong reports in support of the care, this may strengthen their resolve, making settlement more difficult, and, in some cases, impossible.

Sometimes, the medical professional being sued may simply refuse to settle the case, believing it will reflect badly on his or her reputation. Some defendants honestly feel they did nothing wrong and that the care they provided was in keeping with the standard of care. These defendants may wish to be vindicated at trial. In those circumstances, there is little that can be done to settle the case. No one can force a defendant to settle, and everyone is entitled to their day in court, should they so desire.

PARTIES CANNOT AGREE ON AMOUNT OF SETTLEMENT

Some cases are taken to trial because the parties cannot agree on the amount of compensation that the defendant should pay to the plaintiff. If there is a significant discrepancy between the parties regarding the value of the claim, then a trial may be necessary. Given the risks of a trial, this situation usually only develops when the amount the defendant is willing to pay is vastly less than what the plaintiff will accept.

For many medical malpractice plaintiffs, the prospect of a trial is terrifying and one they want to avoid if at all possible. Indeed, no trial is without risks and challenges, and birth injury trials are exceptionally complex and challenging. That is precisely why it is crucial that the lawyer advancing the case have extensive knowledge and experience in this domain.

BILA lawyers have built their reputations, first and foremost as trial lawyers with strong, proven track records of success. The resources, trial experience, and expertise brought to bear by BILA lawyers in birth injury trials is second to none. If your case is taken to trial, you can rest assured that you will receive the highest calibre of legal representation.

CHAPTER 10

HOW DOES THE COURT PROCESS WORK?

by Chris Wullum

After 15 hours of labour, Sarah is about to start pushing when her doctor realizes the baby's shoulder is blocking the birth canal. Sarah is told not to push and that they must deliver the baby immediately. Her doctor informs her that if they cannot change the baby's position after one attempt, Sarah will have to have an emergency c-section. The doctor applies downward traction on the fetal head and successfully dislodges the shoulder. Sarah is able to deliver the baby vaginally; however, the pressure results in a brachial plexus injury, and it is unclear how much damage has been done to her son's arm.

Two years later, Sarah files a malpractice claim to help offset the cost of physical therapy her son now requires. Her BILA lawyer secures experts willing to testify that, should Sarah have had a c-section, her son's injury could have been avoided. Before the case goes to trial, both parties agree to a facilitated mediation session, during which a settlement is agreed on.

Once the decision has been made, after investigation and consultation with your lawyer, that there is merit in pursuing a claim for compensation and damages related to a birth injury, the court process starts with filing the lawsuit.

The court process can be complex and unfamiliar to someone who has never been through it before. It is sometimes referred to as the litigation process. Most people will have seen segments or examples of the court process on television and in movies. While some of what you may have seen is an accurate representation of what occurs, the reality is that there are many more steps to the court process than you will see on screen, and a lot of work occurs in between the various steps of the court process. Your BILA lawyer will be familiar with, and experienced in, guiding you through your lawsuit.

The trial is one of the last stages of the court process and only occurs if a negotiated settlement of the case cannot be achieved at an earlier stage. Anyone entering the litigation process should be prepared for the possibility of a trial as there is never any guarantee that a case can be resolved simply through negotiation and settlement. Having said that, BILA lawyers meticulously prepare each and every case with the trial in mind to ensure that the defence appreciates the risks to them of proceeding to trial. In this way, BILA lawyers increase the likelihood of settlement before trial. Where trial is necessary, your BILA lawyer has the training and experience to proceed with the trial.

It is important when starting the court process that you have an understanding of the various steps and an overview of what to expect. Your BILA lawyer will be able to navigate the court process in a way that should bring some ease and understanding for you in what can be a difficult, confusing, and even stressful experience.

Every Court jurisdiction has its own Court Rules that set out specific details on how each step in the litigation process should occur and over what timeframe. There are many similarities in the Court Rules between provinces and territories, but each jurisdiction will have its own subtle differences. For that reason, it is always best to consult with the lawyer in the province in which your baby was born. For the purposes of this chapter, we'll set out the typical steps in the court process that exist generally across Canada throughout the various jurisdictions.

Statement of Claim

Pursuing a lawsuit starts with the filing of a formal court document that names the parties to the lawsuit and sets out the basic allegations, or material facts, about what occurred. It also offers a description of the various types of damages being sought against the parties being sued. This initiating document is usually referred to as a Statement of Claim or Notice of Civil Claim, depending on the jurisdiction.

In the Statement of Claim, you are seeking damages and are known as the *plaintiffs*. The parties being sued (e.g., doctors, nurses, hospitals, midwives) and contesting the claim for damages are known as the *defendants*.

In birth injury claims, given that the person who has suffered the injuries is a minor under the age of eighteen and likely has a disability, the claim will usually need to be commenced through a *litigation guardian*(s). A ligation guardian is essentially someone who will act in the interests of the infant plaintiff in pursuing the claim, making decisions and giving instructions in respect of the claim on their behalf. In most cases, this would typically be the parents or other legal guardian of the child.

Statement of Defence

Once served with the Statement of Claim, the defendants will then have a period of time, which will be specified in the Court Rules or through agreement of counsel, to file with the court a written response to the claim in a document known as a *Statement of Defence* or *Response to Civil Claim,* depending on the jurisdiction. Similar to the claim, this defence or response will set out the basic responses of the defendants to the allegations made by the plaintiffs in their claim.

THE DISCOVERY STAGE

After the Statement of Claim and Statements of Defence have been delivered, the next significant step in the litigation process is usually referred to as the *discovery stage.* The purpose of this stage is to allow the parties in the case to obtain a greater understanding of the facts and details of the opposing party's case through the disclosure and discovery of documents and testimony. This allows each side the opportunity to better understand and assess the opposing side's case, to know what case they must answer to at trial, and to promote the possibility of settlement through the disclosure of evidence. This is done through direct questioning of the parties by opposing lawyers and through disclosing relevant documents.

There are generally two parts to the discovery stage in a court proceeding. The first involves documentary discovery, in which the parties compile a list of all of the relevant documents that they have in their possession, power, or control. This list of documents is known in most jurisdictions as an Affidavit of Documents, as the party will attach the list of documents to a sworn Affidavit confirming that the list is a full and proper description of all such documents in their possession, power, or control.

In a birth injury case, such relevant documents will usually include the medical charts and records concerning the infant plaintiff, starting from the time of the incident in question up to present date. It will also usually include other documents such as therapy, counselling, or school records, as well as documents related to the caregivers and their circumstances. Documents to be disclosed include the medical records of the mom and any other records that might be relevant to the claims being made (e.g., tax returns, employment records, insurance policies).

It should also be noted that evidence disclosed in the discovery phase is protected by a principle known as the *implied undertaking rule*. This rule prevents an opposing party from using evidence disclosed in the discovery phase for anything other than the specific litigation.

The second aspect of the discovery stage is generally known as *examinations for discovery* or questioning. Examinations for discovery are a vitally important part of a birth injury lawsuit. It is part of the discovery stage, in which the lawyers may ask questions and seek answers under oath from the opposing parties to the case. This questioning typically takes place in a boardroom with a court reporter or stenographer present to transcribe what is said. Counsel for the party being examined is present with their client and has the right to object to any questions asked by opposing counsel that are irrelevant or otherwise inappropriate for discovery. There is no judge present and, as a result, usually occurs in a slightly more informal manner than how evidence might be presented at trial.

The purpose of an examination for discovery is to allow each party to better understand the evidence of the opposing party's case and to seek admissions of facts and evidence of the case. In a birth injury case, counsel for the plaintiffs have the opportunity to ask questions of each doctor or nurse named as a defendant in the claim. Conversely, counsel for the defendants are entitled to question the adult plaintiffs, usually the parents or other guardian or caregiver, about their recollection of events that led to the injuries, as well as questions relevant to the claim for compensation and damages.

An examination for discovery can take several hours (or even days), depending on the facts and complexity of the case. It is important that you spend time with your lawyer in advance of examinations for discovery to prepare so that you know what to expect in the form of possible questions from opposing counsel.

The examinations for discovery are an important step in the litigation process as it is an opportunity for each side to learn many specific factual details of the opposing side's case. It allows counsel to further assess the evidence of the case and even allows them to assess how the person being examined may present as a witness at trial. It aids counsel for the parties in assessing the relative strengths and weaknesses of the claim or defence, and, therefore, can play an important part in influencing settlement of a case.

EXPERT REPORTS

Another important step in the litigation process of a birth injury claim involves obtaining and providing expert reports that set out the expert opinion evidence relied upon by each side. As already discussed in this book, an important aspect of any birth injury malpractice case comes from obtaining and relying upon experts who provide opinions on various medical issues and damages issues relevant to the case. As part of the litigation process, the parties need to disclose written reports that set out details of the expert opinions they would rely upon at trial. Each jurisdiction will have its own specific Court Rules governing the form, content, and timing of such written expert reports.

PRE-TRIAL CONFERENCES WITH A JUDGE

In most jurisdictions, once the discovery stage is complete, the court process will require counsel for the parties to meet with a Judge from the Court to discuss the status of the litigation. Such meetings will have different names depending on the court's jurisdiction, but are often referred to as *pre-trial conferences* or *case management conferences*.

The judge at such conferences will discuss the issues and facts of the case with counsel often with a view to determining if there is any possibility of a settlement or if the case needs to proceed to a trial to be decided.

MEDIATION

In some jurisdictions, there is a mandatory mediation process required of the parties to see if they can reach an agreement for a settlement. Even without a requirement for mediation, it is also open to the parties to voluntarily agree to use mediation to discuss and seek a settlement to the case.

The purpose of mediation is to involve the services of a trained third party, called the mediator, who facilitates a discussion of settlement between the parties. In some jurisdictions, the mediator can be a Judge of the Court who will act as a mediator for the parties. In those instances, the judge that acts as a mediator would not act as the judge at the trial of the matter if it did not settle through the mediation process. Whether the parties can reach a settlement of the claim through discussions at a pre-trial, case conference, or mediation depends on the willingness of the each party to negotiate and try to reach an agreement without the necessity of a trial.

The value of a settlement is often measured by how each party views the strengths and weaknesses of their case and their willingness to negotiate and seek a compromised resolution of it.

TRIAL

If the parties cannot achieve a settlement of the case, either through their own negotiations or through the assistance of a mediator or judge, the case will proceed to a trial for determination. A trial is the formal court proceeding where evidence, both documentary and oral testimony from witnesses, is presented to a judge or jury who will then make a decision of whether the claim succeeds, and, if so, what damages should be paid to the plaintiffs by the defendants.

In some jurisdictions a birth trauma case may be tried in front of a jury of six people. This occurs only rarely, usually because it is thought by many lawyers that these cases are too complex for a jury of lay people. On the other hand, some lawyers feel that juries are adequately equipped to handle cases of this nature.

In birth injury cases, trials usually last several weeks to months. Given their complex nature, there will often be many witnesses that are required to give oral testimony to the court and volumes of documents to present.

A trial will usually proceed with the plaintiffs going first to present their evidence in support of their case. This will include calling each of their witnesses to give testimony to the judge or jury. Typically the parents and other family of the infant plaintiff will be called as witnesses to give their recollection of events and to provide information and descriptions of the plaintiff's injuries. There may be other witnesses called, such as treating doctors and other caregivers and therapists. Witnesses will also include the various experts retained on the case by plaintiffs' counsel to provide their opinion evidence to the court.

The counsel calling the witness to the stand to give testimony will question them in what is known as a *direct examination*. Counsel for the opposing party is then entitled to *cross-examine* the witness in an attempt challenge or impugn the witness' evidence.

In a birth injury malpractice case, some of the most important witnesses will be the expert witnesses called by both parties. Typically, there will be several expert witnesses called by each party at a birth injury trial—therefore, the evidence of these various experts can take many days or weeks to present.

Once the plaintiffs have presented all their evidence, the defendants will be given their opportunity to lead their own evidence, including calling their witnesses and filing any additional documents they wish to place into evidence. Your lawyer will have the opportunity to cross-examine each witness called to testify by the defence.

Once all of the witnesses have been called and all of the evidence has been presented, counsel for the parties will be entitled to summarize their facts and arguments to the judge or jury, in what is known as the *closing arguments* or *submissions*.

The judge or jury is then tasked with making a decision as to who wins or loses the case and assessing the quantum of damages being sought. Where the case is tried by a judge, he or she will often take time, sometimes several weeks or several months, to reflect on the evidence and argument of the parties at trial before rendering his or her decision. This is known as the Court *reserving judgment*. The judge will then usually issue his or her decision by way of written reasons that detail the basis for the decision, including the facts and legal arguments that were accepted and relied upon by the judge in reaching that decision.

APPEALS

In some instances, the decision of the judge following trial may still not be the end of the court process. The unsuccessful party has a right to appeal the decision of the trial judge to the Court of Appeal in the jurisdiction where the claim commenced.

An appeal is usually heard by a panel of three Appellate Judges, and the hearing consists of legal argument by counsel. Generally, no new evidence or testimony is permitted to be given to the Court of Appeal unless special permission is granted.

From a Court of Appeal decision, an unsuccessful party's only means of further challenge to the decision is to seek leave to appeal to the Supreme Court of Canada, the highest level of court in our country. *Seeking leave* means the party wishing to appeal must first obtain permission from the Supreme Court to pursue such a further appeal. The Supreme Court of Canada rarely grants leave to appeal, as it generally only hears a limited number of cases and looks to consider issues that may be of general or wider public importance.

The court process can be a lengthy one, especially as birth injury cases are complex and involve many medical issues, damages issues, experts, and medical charts and records. There are many stages and aspects to a lawsuit that require a great deal of work, strategy, preparation, and skill. The guidance of a skilled litigation counsel with experience in birth injury cases is therefore crucial for navigating the court process.

AFTER THE TRIAL: NEXT STEPS

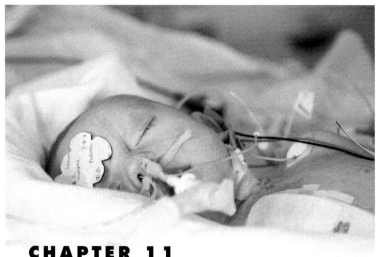

CHAPTER 11

WHAT OTHER STEPS CAN I TAKE?

Whether or not you receive legal advice that a lawsuit is warranted, you may wish to pursue other steps against a doctor or hospital. In general, there are two main avenues of complaint/ investigation:

1. Complaint to the physician's professional regulatory association

2. Complaint to the hospital/health region

While these processes do not typically involve any possibility of financial compensation, you may wish to proceed through one or both of these processes as an alternative to, or in addition to, the litigation process.

In this chapter, we will address the process for both of these processes, as well as the interplay between these administrative processes and the litigation process and applicable time limitations.

This information is intended to provide a general overview and cannot be relied upon to be accurate in every situation. Each province has its own College of Physicians and Surgeons, the statutory self-regulating body responsible for (among other things) licensing physicians, investigating complaints made against physicians, and, in appropriate circumstances, disciplining physicians for conduct determined to be inappropriate. Similarly, while each health region will have some type of internal investigation process to assess complaints, the process will vary by province and health region. As such, if either of these are avenues that you wish to consider, you will need to either speak to your lawyer about the processes in your own province or conduct some inquiries to determine the appropriate steps to take.

THE PROFESSIONAL REGULATORY COMPLAINT PROCESS

Most health-care practitioners, including physicians, nurses, chiropractors, pharmacists, and dentists are members of self-regulating professions. This means that the provincial government does not directly regulate these professions but instead has established a legislative framework under which these professions regulate their own members.

In most jurisdictions, physicians are licensed and regulated by a College of Physicians and Surgeons. The links to the websites of the various Canadian Colleges of Physicians and Surgeons can be found in the Resource section of this book. Each website will typically provide an overview of the complaint process in that jurisdiction and will often provide a copy of the form that is required to be completed if you wish to make a complaint against a physician.

Depending on your particular circumstances, it may be appropriate to initiate a complaint to the College of Physicians and Surgeons in your province (or the professional body of the particular health-care practitioner with whom you have a concern). There are certain cases in which a complaint to a professional body is particularly warranted. These would include situations of unprofessional or unethical conduct, or one in which the physician or other health-care practitioner has exhibited a serious lack of skill or knowledge.

When you initiate a complaint to a professional regulatory association, you will typically be required to complete a complaints form and to sign an authorization form permitting the association to obtain the relevant medical records. While the process may vary somewhat between associations, upon receiving the complaint, the association will typically request a summary from each of the involved practitioners as to the details of the events and their responses to any specific questions you have raised. In most situations, you will receive a copy of these responses, together with the assessment of the professional regulatory association as to the resolution of your complaint.

In some situations, the regulatory body may elect to refer the complaint to a competency committee or inquiry committee in order to assess whether some form of discipline or practice conditions should be imposed. These committees may make further inquiries through correspondence, interviews, or a more formal hearing.

In the vast majority of cases, a complaint to a professional regulatory association does not lead to disciplinary action against the health-care practitioner. However, you may feel that it is important to ensure the regulatory association is aware of your concerns, in the event that there has been a pattern of behaviour with the particular medical practitioner involved. It is often the case that obtaining additional details as to the relevant events through the professional regulatory complaint process can provide a better understanding of what might have led to a negative outcome and can help you come to terms with the events.

HOSPITAL/HEALTH REGION ADMINISTRATIVE COMPLAINT INVESTIGATION PROCESS

In most provinces, hospitals are operated and administered by a health region or health authority. Each region/authority will typically have an internal complaints or administrative investigative process available for patients who have concerns with the care provided to patients at that facility. This may be a Quality Services department, Patient Relations department, through a Patient Advocate, or Client Representative. In most cases, you can determine the general process by looking at the website of the relevant health region.

In most of these facilities or health regions, this internal complaints process is intended to respond to patient concerns and also to ensure quality improvement within the facility/region. While the process will vary from region to region, it is typical that once a complaint is received, the Client Representative (or other similar individual) makes inquiries of involved staff, together with the appropriate department heads. In some instances, you or your family will be invited to attend a meeting of the relevant individuals. Often, a consolidated written response is provided to you in response to the concerns you have raised. In some rare instances, this process may result in disciplinary action or termination of staff. More commonly, it may lead to a change in policy or protocol to improve patient outcome if similar circumstances arise in the future.

INTERPLAY BETWEEN ADMINISTRATIVE PROCESSES AND THE LITIGATION PROCESS

In many cases, clients elect to pursue all three of these available processes (professional regulatory complaint, hospital or health region administrative investigation, and litigation). These processes are not mutually exclusive.

While there is legislation in place in most provinces that prohibit the use of information arising from a professional regulatory complaints process or health region quality assurance process in the course of litigation, and while this does mean that any responses received from the physicians, College, and/or health region cannot be used directly as evidence in any litigation that may follow, the information can certainly be helpful on an indirect basis and can provide assistance to your lawyer in investigating whether litigation is warranted in your situation.

It is important to note that the only process through which you can seek financial compensation is the litigation process.

APPLICABLE TIME LIMITATIONS

While in all provinces there is a legislated limitation date by which any court action must be brought, there are not typically any time limitations with respect to administrative complaints. You may choose to initiate those complaint processes at the same time as you initiate an investigation process with your lawyer, or you may wait and do so once it is determined whether a lawsuit is possible. In any case, it is important to be mindful of the fact that there will be a limitation period applicable to any lawsuit. It is essential that you discuss that with your lawyer at the earliest possible opportunity to ensure that the limitation is not missed.

CHAPTER 12

WHAT LEGAL FEES HAVE TO BE PAID?

by Aleks Mladenovic

Cheryl was in labour for over 35 hours before her doctor performed a c-section. At birth, the baby was blue. A medical team managed to get the baby to start breathing again, and Cheryl and her husband Greg were able to see their son before they took him to the NICU for further testing. But minutes later, Cheryl experienced a postpartum haemorrhage. Doctors were unable to stop the bleeding, and Cheryl died.

As a single father, Greg is worried about legal fees that might arise if he pursues a medical malpractice claim. A BILA lawyer reassures him that he does not need to pay up front, and that the fee would be taken from the settlement. Greg decides to go forward with his claim and is successful in receiving a settlement. While the money will not bring his wife back, it will help Greg provide a future for their son.

Your lawyer will devote a huge amount of time, effort, and skill in pursuing your case over a number of years. As well, your lawyer will have to wait for compensation, like you will, at the end of the case. Importantly, the substantial investment made by your lawyer will not be rewarded unless there is a recovery of damages.

COSTS OF THE PRELIMINARY INVESTIGATION

Before proceeding with a claim, your BILA lawyer will conduct a detailed preliminary investigation, described earlier in this book. This preliminary investigation can result in considerable expense. Most of the time, your BILA lawyer will agree to obtain the relevant records for a preliminary assessment of the merit of your case without any payment from you. In some cases, your BILA lawyer may request a monetary deposit to conduct this investigation. The size of the deposit will depend on the complexity of the issues, the volume of medical records, the number of experts that must be retained, and other anticipated expenses associated with investigating the case.

If your lawyer agrees to proceed with your case under a contingency fee agreement (CFA), you will not be required to pay a deposit. However, a CFA will not be appropriate in all cases. Again, these decisions are made on a case-by case basis.

LEGAL FEES PAYABLE AT THE CONCLUSION OF THE CASE

Whether the case is concluded by a settlement or trial verdict, your lawyer will collect his or her legal fees at the conclusion of the case.

BILA lawyers handle birth injury claims differently than many lawyers in Canada. In particular, BILA lawyers strive for early, efficient, and optimal resolution of birth injury claims, wherever possible. We achieve this by building the medical and economic evidence in your case at the earliest opportunity with the help of quality experts. If a trial is necessary, BILA lawyers have the skill, experience, and reputation to ensure your claim has the best chance of succeeding. The fees charged by BILA lawyers are designed to be fair and reasonable, based on our expertise, the results we obtain, and the sophisticated hands-on approach we take to each and every case.

Although every province has different rules for how legal fees are awarded, a plaintiff who is successful in a lawsuit will ordinarily recover from the defendants an amount for damages as well as some contribution towards legal fees. This is true whether there is an out-of-court settlement or a trial verdict. The contributions to your legal fees made by the defendants are called *partial indemnity costs*. Partial indemnity costs are intended to cover part, but not all of the legal fees you will have to pay to your lawyer. You will still be responsible for paying the balance of the legal fees.

The portion of legal fees you pay to your lawyer at the conclusion of the case is referred to as *solicitor-and-client fees*. The solicitor-and-client fees are taken from the settlement funds or the trial award, depending on how the case was resolved. Solicitor-and-client fees usually represent a pre-arranged percentage of the total damages amount.

In some cases, the other side will have to pay a higher percentage of your legal fees. The legal fees paid by the other side at this higher scale are referred to as *substantial indemnity costs* and are usually only awarded if the case goes to trial. Where this occurs, the amount of the solicitor-and-client fees you will have to pay will be lower.

In cases involving children or individuals who lack capacity to instruct counsel or understand the process of litigation, a litigation guardian will be appointed to act on their behalf. In most cases, the litigation guardian will be a parent or close family member. The litigation guardian is required to act in the best interests of the child or person under a disability. Any proposed settlement in these cases will require the oversight and approval of a judge in the province where the action was commenced.

In addition to overseeing and approving the amount of the settlement, the court will review and scrutinize the solicitor-and-client fees, which are to be paid by the minor plaintiff or party under a disability. In this way, the court will ensure that both the settlement and the legal fees are fair and in the best interests of the child or party under a disability. Your BILA lawyer will navigate you through this process and will prepare all of the necessary materials for court approval of any proposed settlement.

There can be cost consequences to losing a case at trial. BILA lawyers work tirelessly to ensure you receive a favourable result. If the case proceeds to trial and the judge prefers the defence's expert evidence to the plaintiff's expert evidence, your case may be dismissed. Should that occur, the court may order you to pay partial indemnity costs to the opposing side. Your BILA lawyer will work closely with you to ensure that does not happen. Our past experience, while not necessarily predictive of future outcomes, has demonstrated that this outcome is extremely rare for BILA lawyers.

FINAL NOTE

Every parent wishes for nothing more than a healthy child. When the unimaginable happens around birth and a child is injured, a parent's love is no less, but it changes everything. There are times when these things happen without fault—the birth process can be a risky one. Indeed, that is most often the case. Tragically, there are also times when a child's injury was entirely avoidable. It is then that a BILA lawyer can assist you and your family to meet the substantial obligations involved in ensuring that your child is looked after. Getting a big settlement for your child does not undo the wrong, but many parents agree that a good settlement is almost as life-altering as the original injury.

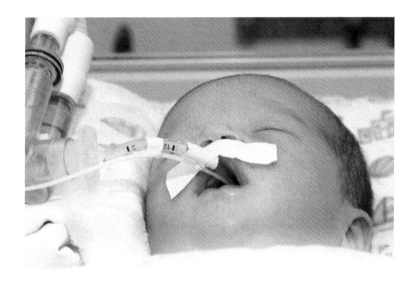

STEP-BY-STEP CHECK LIST FOR BIRTH INJURY MEDICAL MALPRACTICE SUITS

This checklist is intended to provide you with a helpful overview of recommended steps you should take if you think that your child may have been injured by birth trauma.

STEP 1. CONTACT A BILA LAWYER (OR SOME EQUALLY QUALIFIED LAWYER).

☐ Prepare a detailed chronology that includes:

___ Information about your own health (e.g., hypertension, diabetes)

___ Information about your experience during pregnancy

___ Details about who provided medical care during your pregnancy

__Your recollection of events surrounding your labour and the delivery of your child

__ Details about who the health-caregivers were for you and your child

__ The names and addresses of everyone involved in your care and the care of your child

__ Details concerning your child's condition and the medical investigations and care provided to your child to date

STEP 2. MEET WITH YOUR LAWYER.

☐ Provide him or her with your chronology and discuss your case

☐ Ask the lawyer about their experience in acting in cases like yours

☐ Ask the lawyer what the issues are

☐ Ask the lawyer about how he or she gets paid and contingency fee arrangement details

☐ Make sure that the lawyer will do a thorough investigation into the merits of your case before starting a lawsuit

☐ Satisfy yourself that the lawyer understands obstetrical and newborn medical issues

☐ Make sure the lawyer knows the significance and importance of the fetal heart tracing

☐ Make sure that the very first step the lawyer plans to take is to obtain the labour and delivery records, fetal heart tracing, and newborn records to evaluate the merit of your case

☐ Make sure the lawyer has a good understanding of the nature of your baby's injury and the damages that might result

STEP 3. RETAIN YOUR LAWYER.

After you have decided to retain a lawyer to act for you and your child, you should feel comfortable in relying on the lawyer to:

☐ Complete a thorough investigation of your case

☐ Sit down with you to discuss the details of your case and the theory of liability

☐ Explain the basis for your case in plain language

☐ Ensure that there is a reasonable basis for alleging a breach of the standard of care and causation before involving you in a lawsuit

☐ Keep you informed through meetings, telephone calls, letters, and emails on all important developments in your case

☐ Gather up all relevant medical documentation

☐ Meet with you in person and prepare you thoroughly for examination for discovery or questioning

☐ Build your case on damages through the retention of appropriate experts

☐ Attempt to negotiate a settlement of your case only when fully prepared and when there is a clear medical prognosis for your child

☐ Fully prepare for mediation and, if necessary, trial

☐ Generally, to conduct your case in a manner that is entirely focused on the best interests of your child

RESOURCES

FOUNDING MEMBERS OF THE BIRTH INJURY LAWYERS ALLIANCE

Mr. Richard Halpern
Ontario
richard@bila.ca

Mr. Paul McGivern
British Columbia
paul@bila.ca

Mr. John A. McKiggan Q.C.
Atlantic Canada
john@bila.ca

Mr. Joe Miller Q.C.
Alberta
joe@bila.ca

Mr. Ken Ready Q.C.
Saskatchewan
ken@bila.ca

Mr. Chris Wullum
Manitoba
chris@bila.ca

CEREBRAL PALSY RESOURCES

There are many local organizations that provide services and supports for families of children living with cerebral palsy. For a list of organizations in your area, please contact the BILA lawyer in your province

CP ASSOCIATIONS BY PROVINCE

The Cerebral Palsy Association in Alberta (CPAA)
 cpalberta.com

CPAA is a registered non-profit organization that supports people affected by cerebral palsy and other disabilities in Alberta, whose mission is to enrich and support the lives of children and adults with cerebral palsy and other disabilities through programs and services.

Cerebral Palsy Association of BC (CPABC)
 bccerebralpalsy.com

CPABC is a non-profit organization that advocates for, and provides resources and support to, people with cerebral palsy and their families.

Cerebral Palsy Association of Manitoba (CPAM)
 cerebralpalsy.mb.ca

CPAM is an independent non-profit association that offers information, referrals, support, and advocacy to anyone affected with CP and to those interested in, or working with, people affected by CP.

Ontario Federation for Cerebral Palsy (OFCP)
 ofcp.ca

OFCP is a non-profit charitable organization dedicated to supporting people with cerebral palsy in Ontario, with the goal of supporting independence, inclusion, choice, and full integration into the community.

The Cerebral Palsy Foundation (Saint John) Inc.
cpfsj.ca

This non-profit organization represents persons with cerebral palsy across New Brunswick by providing financial assistance, general information about cerebral palsy, and support services to its members.

Cerebral Palsy Association of Newfoundland and Labrador
cerebralpalsynl.com

This is a registered non-profit organization committed to improving the lives of people affected by cerebral palsy and other disabilities across the province by promoting awareness, acceptance, and understanding.

The PEI Cerebral Palsy Association
peicpa.com

This organization advocates on behalf of persons with cerebral palsy and their families and works to raise awareness in society of the abilities of individuals with CP.

Halifax Regional Cerebral Palsy Association
hrcpa.ca

This registered charity has as its main objective the betterment of life for its members and those in mainland Nova Scotia who are living with cerebral palsy.

Saskatchewan Cerebral Palsy Association
saskcp.ca

This is a registered non-profit organization that supports individuals with cerebral palsy and other disabilities in Saskatchewan by promoting awareness and education.

NATIONAL AND INTERNATIONAL RESOURCES

Kids Brain Health Network
  neurodevnet.ca

Kids Brain Health is the new name of NeuroDevNet, the first trans-Canada initiative to focus on improving diagnosis, treatment, and support for families raising children with brain-based disabilities.

Canadian Cerebral Palsy Sports Association (CCPSA)
  ccpsa.ca

The CCPSA is an athlete-focused national organization administering and governing sport opportunities targeted to athletes with CP and related disabilities.

CanChild Centre for Childhood Disability Research
  canchild.ca/en

CanChild is a non-profit research and education centre focused on improving the lives of children and youth with disabilities and their families.

Canadian Disability Resources (CDRS)
  disabilityresources.ca

CDRS is a charitable organization, with the goal of promoting health by providing recycled medical equipment to needy persons with physical disabilities and by developing educational materials and resources for persons with physical disabilities.

Reaching for the Stars: A Foundation of Hope for Children with Cerebral Palsy (RFTS Inc.)
  reachingforthestars.org

RFTS is a non-profit pediatric Cerebral Palsy foundation led by parents, with a focus on the prevention, treatment, and cure of cerebral palsy.

Cerebral Palsy International Research Foundation
cpirf.org

CPIRF is a not-for-profit organization dedicated to funding research and educational activities directly relevant to discovering the cause, cure, and evidence-based care for those with cerebral palsy and related developmental disabilities.

United Cerebral Palsy
ucp.org

This is an international non-profit charitable organization, and hub for local affiliated cerebral palsy associations that educates, advocates, and provides support services to ensure a life without limits for people with cerebral palsy.

Convention on the Rights of Persons with Disabilities
un.org/disabilities/convention/conventionfull.shtml

Canada is a signatory country of this convention, which sets out basic fundamental rights of persons with disabilities.

NATIONAL AND PROVINCIAL MEDICAL REGULATORY AUTHORITIES

National

Royal College of Physicians and Surgeons of Canada

royalcollege.ca/rcsite/home-e

Provincial

College of Physicians and Surgeons of British Columbia

300-669 Howe Street

Vancouver, BC V6C 0B4

Phone: 604-733-7758 or 1-800-461-3008

Fax: 604-733-3503

registration@cpsbc.ca

College of Physicians and Surgeons of Alberta

2700 Telus Plaza South | 10020 — 100 Street NW

Edmonton AB T5J 0N3

Phone: 780-423-4764 or 1-800-561-3899

Fax: 780-420-0651

info@cpsa.ab.ca

College of Physicians and Surgeons of Saskatchewan

101–2174 Airport Drive

Saskatoon SK S7L 6M6

Phone: 306-244-7355 or 1-800-667-1668

Fax: 306-244-0090

cpssinfo@cps.sk.ca

College of Physicians and Surgeons of Manitoba

1000 - 1661 Portage Avenue

Winnipeg MB R3J 3T7

Phone: 204-774-4344

Fax: 204-774-0750

TheRegistrar@cpsm.mb.ca

College of Physicians and Surgeons of Ontario

80 College Street

Toronto ON M5G 2E2

Phone: 416-967-2603 or 1-800-268-7096

feedback@cpso.on.ca

Collège des médecins du Québec

2170, boulevard René-Lévesque Ouest

Montréal QC H3H 2T8

Phone: 514-933-4441 ou 1-888-MÉDECIN

Fax: 514-933-3112

info@cmq.org

College of Physicians and Surgeons of New Brunswick

1 Hampton Road, Suite 300

Rothesay NB E2E 5K8

Phone: 506-849-5050 or 1-800-667-4641

Fax: 506-849-5069

info@cpsnb.org

College of Physicians and Surgeons of Nova Scotia

7071 Bayers Road, Suite 5005

Halifax NS B3L 2C2

Phone: 902-422-5823 or 1-877-282-7767

Fax: 902-422-5035

registration@cpsns.ns.ca

College of Physicians and Surgeons of Prince Edward Island

199 Grafton Street

Charlottetown PE C1A 1L2

Phone: 902-566-3861

Fax: 902-566-3861

College of Physicians and Surgeons of Newfoundland & Labrador

139 Water St, Suite 603

St. John's NL A1C 1B2

Phone: 709-726-8546

Fax: 709-726-4725

cpsnl@cpsnl.ca

Yukon Medical Council

c/o Registrar of Medical Practitioners

Box 2703 C-18

Whitehorse YT Y1A 2C6

Phone: 867-667-3774

Fax: 867-393-6483

ymc@gov.yk.ca

Health and Social Services

Government of the Northwest Territories

PO Box 1320

Yellowknife NT X1A 2L9

Phone: 867-920-8058

Fax: 867-873-0484

professional_licensing@gov.nt.ca

Department of Health and Social Services

Government of Nunavut

P.O. Box 1000 Station 200

Iqaluit, Nunavut X0A 0H0

Phone: 1-877-212-6438

info@gov.nu.ca

OTHER LINKS

BILA website

Bila.ca

The Canadian Bar Association

www.cba.org/Home

Birth Trauma Canada

birthtraumacanada.org/

Directory of Canadian Certified Counsellors

ccpa-accp.ca/find-a-canadian-certified-counsellor/

Being a Caregiver (Service Canada)

servicecanada.gc.ca/eng/lifeevents/caregiver.shtml

Disability Benefits (Government of Canada)

canada.ca/en/services/benefits/disability.html

WA